Transitioning to the Prototype Church

Book 2 of the Prototype Church Series

The Church is in a Season of Profound of Transition

Bill Vincent

© 2016 by Bill Vincent.

All rights reserved. No part of this book may be reproduced, stored in a retrieval system or transmitted in any form or by any means without the prior written permission of the publishers, except by a reviewer who may quote brief passages in a review to be printed in a newspaper, magazine or journal.

Paperback: 978-1-60796-983-9

Hardcover: 978-1-365-82350-3

PUBLISHED BY REVIVAL WAVES OF GLORY BOOKS & PUBLISHING

www.revivalwavesofgloryministries.com

Litchfield, IL

Printed In the United States of America

Table of Contents

Chapter One Knowing the Opposition 4
Chapter Two Breakthrough is Upon Us 15
Chapter Three A New Church Arises In Revelation 22
Chapter Four A New Church Arises In Confrontation 33
Chapter Five A New Church Arises In Transformation 57
Chapter Six A New Church Arises In Manifestations 75
Chapter Seven The Royal Process 81
Chapter Eight Kingly Character 91
Chapter Nine The New Church 99
Chapter Ten The Fire of God's Glory 106
Chapter Eleven Transformed Mind 112
Chapter Twelve A New Level 123
Chapter Thirteen The Key to the Nation 127
Chapter Fourteen Living in the Fire 131
Chapter Fifteen Wealth of the Nations 137
Chapter Sixteen AWARENESS of God 141
Chapter Seventeen Creative Thoughts 156
Chapter Eighteen Rise Up or Die 178
Chapter Nineteen Rediscovering the Early Pathways 188
Chapter Twenty The Fire Without Being Burned 199
Chapter Twenty One Choosing to Be in God's Plan 204
Chapter Twenty Two The Anointed Eagles Vision 214
Chapter Twenty Three The Warrior Eagle Vision 224
About the Author 236
Recommended Books 237

Chapter One
Knowing the Opposition

If you are experiencing God's power and presence at any level you will see the opposition of the Enemy. This is a day when Breaking Spiritual Strongholds is through knowing the oppositions. We are in a season of transition and it is time to know the enemy. The ground of transition will be contested by the ruthless enemy who will try and frustrate us at every turn. That is why the whole point of times of transition is to increase our dependency upon the Lord. We must learn how to hold on to the majesty and supremacy of Jesus. It is so easy when we are going through change and transition to blame the enemy, to blame people, or to look at a human rationale for our situation.

I believe that God wants to give us a divine rationale because, in my experience with God limited though it may be. I have come to understand that God allows in His wisdom what He could easily prevent by His power. If God is allowing certain things, then we want to know His wisdom.

John 16:12 I have yet many things to say unto you, but ye cannot bear them now.

He was limited in what He could do in their hearts and what He could speak into their lives because of their own perception. The Lord is always trying to raise our perception of what He is doing. That is what we call revelation. That could be said of the Church right now. Deep is calling to deep. I have never known a time when

The Church is in a Season of Profound of Transition

I have felt such a weight of Heaven pressing in on what we are doing. Angelic sightings around the world are on the increase. Demonic manifestations that are more powerful and strange are also on the increase. The supernatural is folding itself layer upon layer on top of the natural. Heaven is desperate to come to earth. There are more intercessors now in the earth than there have ever been as a whole of the Church's entire history. There is a tremendous amount of intercession going up these days. Every church, no matter how small, has someone praying intensely. Many churches are coming into a place of intensity with intercession. It is easy to see that the whole world is shifting. There are deep things happening across the Church, some of which we don't yet understand. I believe there will be some messages coming to the Church that will come by angelic visitation because we won't be able to bear the weight of them. No one will be able to get the weight of revelation by themselves from the Holy Spirit. I believe that we will have angels coming just as we saw in the Scriptures, in both the Old and New Covenants.

Angels are sent to help mankind break through when they cannot break out. They operate at the points where Heaven touches the earth, where significance needs to be broadcast, and where God's plans and purposes need to unfold with dynamic effect. They are ministering spirits sent to give a message or support at a critical time. Their presence is increasing in the earth. This is a truly supernatural time for churches to gain that heavenly cutting edge of spiritual gifting and character. We are breaking new ground and becoming more prophetic in a world going mad with reason. Prophetic churches pass through things ahead of time. This will make us a target for criticism. This will no doubt be good for our humility. Human opposition is designed by God to bring us into grace.

Demonic opposition brings us into greater power. All opposition is designed for our benefit. Human opposition will teach us how to be gracious and merciful. We will learn how to love our enemies, how to pray for people who persecute us, and how to bless those who work against us. Demonic opposition is to teach us how to stand in the authority and the power of the Lord Jesus. It is designed to show us the majesty and supremacy of Jesus and to enable us to learn how to submit to God.

James 4:7, 8 Submit yourselves therefore to God. Resist the devil, and he will flee from you. Draw nigh to God, and he will draw nigh to you. Cleanse *your* hands, *ye* sinners; and purify *your* hearts, *ye* double minded.

Everything that this type of church does is built on progressive truth. Revelation that is unfolding will not be understood by other churches until it is released out in something visible. This takes perseverance on our behalf, so that one day our critics can have fellowship with us in spirit and truth. We need to keep praying over our religious saints that the Lord will open their eyes, that what is invisible and therefore beyond your understanding can be seen and apprehended. The church needs a total change of perspective to operate in the supernatural realm. We cannot indulge in the laws of reason and logic and expect to fight off the demonic. We cannot hear words concerning the future without willingly changing our practices in the present. We will see what God is seeing; speak out what He is saying; and do what only He is doing simply because He wills it. We will have to suspend our disbelief to share the perceptions of the Holy Spirit.

The enemy must be known, isolated, and overcome if we are to move into the realms of God that are unfolding. That is why we need the prophetic. Prophets have a profound love of God and a deep hatred of the enemy. They have always been in the forefront of any battle against untruth, deception, injustice, and oppression. Most of the leaders in the Bible had a strong prophetic dimension to their lives. Many were prophets! Yet the notion in today's churches is that prophets and leadership do not mix. We have a church that does not understand process and growth, largely because the people who understand these realms are not in any place of authority or real influence. Reason has replaced revelation. I love reason. I believe that God is reasonable, except when He chooses not to be. Then we need revelation. Words of wisdom are meant to provide us with supernatural reasoning that is not grounded in human logic and intelligence.

The mind must be renewed at times in order to keep pace with God's reasoning. Things that do not make sense in the natural will unfold supernaturally by divine revelation as God communicates at a deeper level of faith and on a higher plane of thought. Our thoughts are not His yet! Real prophetic people naturally interact with God on this level of supernatural understanding by revelation.

Real apostles have the natural capacity in the Spirit to interpret prophetic revelation into a strategy for church response and development. That is why the new prototype of Church will be founded on the partnership between apostles and prophets dependent on the Lord Jesus Christ.

Only a few people understand the process of turning prophetic potential into something actual. It is one matter to have received a prophetic word; it is quite another to see it fulfilled. I personally know many individuals and churches with significant prophetic words spoken over them. All personal prophecy is conditional, whether or not any conditions are implied or stated in the prophecy itself. Conditional prophecy relates to the possibility, not the certainty of fulfillment. It can be delayed or even canceled according to our response as well as by our capacity to align our hearts and lives in lifestyle obedience to the revealed word of God in the Scriptures. There is unconditional prophecy, which relates to God's overall plan for mankind. It may be adjusted but can never be prevented from coming to pass because it depends upon God Himself, not human response. We need perseverance and patience to walk with God and see that word fulfilled according to the Lord's discretion and timing, as well as according to our preparation and placement.

We will need to work with the Holy Spirit to turn our potential into reality. Working with frustration is a key factor in turning our potential into something actual. I like frustrated people. They are one of the hopes of the church. Most people are frustrated because they care about something. However, they have a distinct responsibility to the Holy Spirit to use their frustration for the correct purpose.

If people abuse their relationship with the Holy Spirit, their frustration is used by the flesh to sow discord, strife, and division. They will become a dissenting voice rather than a positive prophetic utterance. Frustration reveals our true heart and releases an impartation that is either negative and destructive, or positive and empowering. If we intervene between our frustration and God's purpose, we are tampering with the law of cause and effect. People do not guard their thoughts carefully enough, especially when under the pressure of frustration. If we leave our thoughts unguarded, the flesh can take what the Lord wants to do.

We need a genuine respect for cause and effect as a necessary condition for turning frustration into impartation. By choosing God's purpose, we reject the potential for divisiveness to occur. Cause always belongs to God; the effect is whatever is released through the Son. Frustration is sent to change us, to make us more into the image of Jesus; that is cause and effect, stage one. When we allow frustration to cause us to stand in the gap and intercede for others, the effect of which is a release of impartation that empowers and inspires. That is, we arrive at a place of trustworthy servanthood after having passed the test of unselfishness. All fear is implicit in the second, and all love is implicit in the first. The conflict is therefore between love and fear. Do we love God enough to allow Him to fulfill His purpose no matter how much it hurts ours? Do we love other people enough to serve and help them no matter how much we want to be right?

Isaac was not the cause of Abraham's prophetic inheritance to be fulfilled; he was the effect. The cause to fulfill the prophecy over Abraham was only ever going to be God Himself.

Genesis 18:10-19 And he said, I will certainly return unto thee according to the time of life; and, lo, Sarah thy wife shall have a son. And Sarah heard *it* in the tent door, which *was* behind him. Now Abraham and Sarah *were* old *and* well stricken in age; *and* it ceased to be with Sarah after the manner of women. Therefore Sarah laughed within herself, saying, After I am waxed old shall I have pleasure, my lord being old also? And the LORD said unto Abraham, Wherefore did Sarah laugh, saying, Shall I of a surety bear a child, which am old? Is any thing too hard for the LORD? At the time appointed I will return unto thee, according to the time of life, and Sarah shall have a son. Then Sarah denied, saying, I laughed not; for she was afraid. And he said, Nay; but thou didst laugh. And the men rose up from thence, and looked toward Sodom: and Abraham went with them to bring them on the way. And the LORD said, Shall I hide from Abraham that thing which I do; Seeing that Abraham shall surely become a great and mighty nation, and all the nations of the earth shall be blessed in him? For I know him, that he will command his children and his household after him, and they shall keep the way of the LORD, to do justice and judgment; that the LORD may bring upon Abraham that which he hath spoken of him.

Part of our frustration is that we cannot see where our lives fit into the current circumstances unless they change. Can we lay our desire and our hope for significance on the altar of God and trust in Him alone to fulfill it? It is a test a real and great examination of our motives, desires, and true spirit of servanthood. It is here that we will discover whether we will seize the occasion for our own ends or whether we will lay down our lives for the purpose of obedience.

When Abraham was told to offer up Isaac as a sacrifice, it was a major test of his obedience.

Genesis 22:8 And Abraham said, My son, God will provide himself a lamb for a burnt offering: so they went both of them together.

Genesis 22:15-18 And the angel of the LORD called unto Abraham out of heaven the second time, And said, By myself have I sworn, saith the LORD, for because thou hast done this thing, and hast not withheld thy son, thine only *son:* That in blessing I will bless thee, and in multiplying I will multiply thy seed as the stars of the heaven, and as the sand which *is* upon the sea shore; and thy seed shall possess the gate of his enemies; And in thy seed shall all the nations of the earth be blessed; because thou hast obeyed my voice.

We can hold on to our own dream only by letting it go in the service of God. That, perhaps, is one of the lessons of frustration that we all must learn if we are to be true servants of God. His promise and goodness are the cause of our fulfillment, not our desire to take hold of the promise and make it work.

David had to learn a similar lesson in his life with Saul. King Saul had pursued David with every evil intent to prevent his son-in-law from becoming his successor to the throne. When Saul entered the very cave where David and his men were hiding, to relieve himself, he was at their mercy. David's friends urged him to kill Saul, believing that God had ordained it. On that day, David realized that the cause of his inheriting the throne was not the demise of Saul. It was simply the will and power of God to fulfill His own word. The only person who could wreck the cause of God was David himself. In frustration, conflict is inevitable if we are not focused upon God's purpose. Our self-righteous flesh will rise up to prove its point, justifying itself in the process. The effect of our flesh is unproductive and damaging to the cause of God. In frustration we must be ready with our obedience to fulfill the cause of God. Then the effect of our frustration is an impartation of encouragement, prophecy, insight, and blessing. Readiness is a prerequisite for accomplishment. As soon as a state of readiness occurs within us, it will be accompanied by a desire to accomplish the will of God through His Spirit. Readiness is the beginning of confidence.

God knows what He is doing, and we would rather trust His faithfulness to do it than our capacity to understand it. We know that all things become clear in the end. The God who will not explain Himself before the event will reveal His purpose after we have trusted. He does not always speak initially, but He always speaks eventually. By submitting to Him, no matter how we feel, we become ready to do His will. Frustration is either the spark of life that creates a new dimension or the discharge of all that we hold dear. Do not snuff out that spark, but nurture it properly. The current problem in leadership concerns time, motion, and efficiency.

With so many things happening, and with so many claims on our time, it is easier and seemingly more effective to regulate certain situations and people than it is to facilitate and develop them. It is easier to deny than to expedite. People need to understand that, firstly, frustration is an internal matter. It will highlight where and how the Lord wants to change the individual. Leaders need to give them help primarily to rid the people of unhelpful elements.

Psalms 139:23, 24 Search me, O God, and know my heart: try me, and know my thoughts: And see if *there be any* wicked way in me, and lead me in the way everlasting.

We must ensure that our frustration about something is not turned into anything hurtful to others. Once we have allowed the Lord to deal with our own hearts, we are free to pray effectively and to stand in the gap for others.

How we deal with our frustration is a major test of our faithfulness to working with the Holy Spirit. Can He trust us? Are we committed to the fruit of the Holy Spirit or just His gifting? Are we committed to the building up of the Body or to just our own ministry? Frustration is a well-designed test to determine faithfulness and current attitude. It is a privilege to be frustrated. It means, if we handle it properly, if we prove out and achieve what is on God's heart, that a new door in the Spirit realm will open up to us. If we miss the opportunity and our frustration falls into fleshly activity, that door will close on us. It may be some time before the Lord will trust us enough to open that door again. Frustration is the potential to grow and develop. Of course, if we are constantly and continuously frustrated, we will need some form of counseling and possibly deliverance from spiritual negativity, pride, contempt, and arrogance. The flesh will have got the better of us on a regular basis, and now we become a liability. The enemy, not the Holy Spirit, is now monitoring our frustration for the purpose of strife and division, not growth and development. God will change us first through our frustration; then He will change people around us. Frustration will bring everyone and everything into alignment with God's purpose, if we submit to Him. Transition is essential in turning our revelation into experience.

There are two things we really need here. We need a revelation of what frustration is really all about and we must understand that transition is the place where revelation becomes experience to us. Transition is a testing and proving ground.

It is the place between promise and fulfillment where we are tested to see if we can inhabit the place that God wants to give us. The promise made to Adam was that he would rule over the earth and have dominion in it. He was put into the Garden of Eden to see if he could rule over himself. The garden was his transition place a smaller sphere of influence and activity that was designed to be his testing and proving ground. He missed it. We must be honest with ourselves. How many times have we been frustrated? Has anything positive and remarkable ever occurred in those times? If we are blaming others, we have missed the point.

For every finger we point at someone else, there are three pointing back at us. Did those times of frustration lead us to greater impartation, renewed servanthood, or a test passed with flying colors? If not, then these tests will come again. Times of testing are part of the process of turning our potential into something actual. We can tell who are men and women of real substance in God. They are the ones at peace with themselves. They own nothing and yet possess all things. They are not striving, not promoting themselves. They are content to trust God. He puts things into their hands because He trusts them. Their frustration has been redeemed. In its place is a continuous flow of impartation. They have become facilitators for other people. They are not concerned with their own place in the scheme of things. Great servants always have a place. Faithfulness is its own reward.

Chapter Two
Breakthrough is Upon Us

When Transitioning Into a Prototype Church you will see the greatest breakthroughs you have ever seen. Breakthroughs are not always obvious. Many do not recognize their point of origin. Breakthroughs do not begin at the point of discovery. They start much further back than we imagine. They begin at the point where we set ourselves to seek the Lord by extended, intensive prayer with fasting.

Daniel 10:2-4 In those days I Daniel was mourning three full weeks. I ate no pleasant bread, neither came flesh nor wine in my mouth, neither did I anoint myself at all, till three whole weeks were fulfilled. And in the four and twentieth day of the first month, as I was by the side of the great river, which *is* Hiddekel;

Daniel 10:12 Then said he unto me, Fear not, Daniel: for from the first day that thou didst set thine heart to understand, and to chasten thyself before thy God, thy words were heard, and I am come for thy words.

Daniel was not aware of the breakthrough or its point of origin until he was told about it. Breakthroughs occur when we begin to pray in earnest and are recognized after prayer is complete. Daniel stood firm in prayer so that his intercession could be completed before the Lord. Had he given up on prayer, that which had begun on the first day of intercession may not have been completed to the point of recognition at a later time. Everything that God does is birthed through warfare and confrontation. While Daniel was praying, warfare was being conducted over the nation. Daniel was unaware of the battle or even his part in it. He had no idea what his faithful praying had contributed to the heavenly battle.

Wherever Jesus went, He provoked warfare. Demons would cry out, provoked by His presence. Healing and deliverance occurred because of the interaction between His presence and demonic forces. Some people tried to stone Him, others kill Him. If we are praying for His presence to come, provocation will come with Him! We will partake of all the warfare He provokes.

Breakthroughs come in times of warfare and confrontation. If you want me to come to give you breakthrough, you had better know that if you don't have a confrontation while I am there, you will have it soon after I have gone, because that is the nature of breakthrough. You have to have a battle to break through. You have to be in a war to break through. The enemy has to come against you so that you can break through against him. He has to come on to your defense. You also have to go on the offensive so you can break through against him.

In times of war, we will see a side of God that we do not see at any other time. That is why confrontation and warfare are so important. We are not afraid of it; the truth is, we have to get to like it. That doesn't mean that we all become deliriously happy at the thought of spiritual warfare. We can relish the fight once we are in it, but we must count the cost before we start it. Our God is not afraid of anything; nor is He upset or provoked by anything. He is a God of war and He laughs in the face of His enemy, because

God knows who He is in Himself. He has total knowledge of His own identity. He wants to put all the qualities and characteristics of His own warfare nature into the church. However, He only puts them in us on the battlefield. So we have to get on the battlefield! There are a lot of churches that are not even on the battlefield yet. We have to be good enough to be attacked by the devil. Most churches are not good enough to come into real spiritual warfare. The enemy does not have to attack them because they do a pretty good job by themselves! The devil doesn't have to attack a lot of churches. He can simply come in and press a few buttons of the flesh: resentment, bitterness, ambition, pride, arrogance, and unteachable behavior. As long as he can press those buttons, we cannot make it to the same battlefield. We have to win the internal battle before we can win the external one. We have to win the internal battle as individuals. We also have to win it on a corporate level so that we come together as one people with one heart, one mind, and one voice. Then we are ready for real warfare, and then all hell will break loose around us. Then we will find that God will reveal Himself in a way that we never thought possible. The nature and spiritual capacity of a church changes dramatically when the God of battle presents Himself in its midst!

Luke 22:28-30 Ye are they which have continued with me in my temptations. And I appoint unto you a kingdom, as my Father hath appointed unto me; That ye may eat and drink at my table in my kingdom, and sit on thrones judging the twelve tribes of Israel.

Mattew 11:12 And from the days of John the Baptist until now the kingdom of heaven suffereth violence, and the violent take it by force.

In warfare and seasons of trouble, there is a quality of suffering and perseverance that actually births in us a greater anointing to work the works of God. God actually trusts us, because He trusts what He sees of suffering inside our heart and life. We cannot build anything without suffering. So many leaderships are moving away from suffering. Good leadership knows how to suffer; they know about patience and perseverance to stand their ground. People can leave, but the leaders will stand their ground. It is in that time that God learns He can trust us. He bestows something in us. Anytime God has actually increased the anointing upon my life (over the past 22 years), it has come after a time of severe battle, warfare, criticism, or suffering of one kind or another. We suddenly look back and we realize that the grace of God helped us to stand in that time. Then the blessing of God came upon us afterwards and increased the anointing.

1 Timothy 1:12 And I thank Christ Jesus our Lord, who hath enabled me, for that he counted me faithful, putting me into the ministry;

There is a faithfulness there that we are both earning and learning to develop in the heart of the Lord. Each one of us will go through that kind of transition. We need to understand the stages that God will take us through so that we don't run at the critical moment. We are going to have some interesting and critical times in church life where everything is balanced on a knife edge. We will learn about the mind of God as He teaches us to walk by faith and not by sight. We also will receive His goodness and mercy. His mouth will discipline us into the simple obedience of faith at the same time as His heart will comfort us in our distress of learning.

Isaiah 1:18 Come now, and let us reason together, saith the LORD: though your sins be as scarlet, they shall be as white as snow; though they be red like crimson, they shall be as wool.

Proverbs 3:5 Trust in the LORD with all thine heart; and lean not unto thine own understanding.

The issue is if we believe, not if we understand. In the next dimension of church, we must prepare ourselves to walk with the God of the unreasonable. He will call us to do the impossible, to take on projects that are inconceivable to our mindsets. These projects will have their roots in the prophetic. That is why we must nurture the prophetic gift and ministry in our midst. Without it, we cannot become a prophetic church that is able to imagine all that the Lord would want to accomplish in and through us. Without that revelatory rationale to guide and help us, we will miss the grandeur of the wider purposes of God. We will be trying to take a neighborhood while He wants to give us the city. We will be attempting to believe God about the wider locality when He wants to use us as a catalyst to take the nation. We look at our own resources and the scale of the problem in front of us, and we make a rational, intelligent judgment of our chances for pulling it off. If the circumstances look too huge and awesome, we will not even attempt the matter.

Numbers 13:25-33 And they returned from searching of the land after forty days. And they went and came to Moses, and to Aaron, and to all the congregation of the children of Israel, unto the wilderness of Paran, to Kadesh; and brought back word unto them, and unto all the congregation, and shewed them the fruit of the land. And they told him, and said, We came unto the land whither thou sentest us, and surely it floweth with milk and honey; and this *is* the fruit of it. Nevertheless the people *be* strong that dwell in the land, and the cities *are* walled, *and* very great: and moreover we saw the children of Anak there. The Amalekites dwell in the land of the south: and the Hittites, and the Jebusites, and the Amorites, dwell in the mountains: and the Canaanites dwell by the sea, and by the coast of Jordan. And Caleb stilled the people before Moses, and said, Let us go up at once, and possess it; for we are well able to overcome it. But the men that went up with him said, We be not able to go up against the people; for they *are* stronger than we. And they brought up an evil report of the land which they had searched unto the children of Israel, saying, The land, through which we have gone to search it, *is* a land that eateth up the inhabitants thereof; and all the people that we saw in it *are* men of a great stature. And there we saw the giants, the sons of Anak, *which come* of the giants: and we were in our own sight as grasshoppers, and so we were in their sight.

However, when we are moving in faith regarding God's ability, we put a different complexion on things. Like Joshua and Caleb, we will give a report that is full of regard for the anointing of God, even at our own expense.

Numbers 14:7-9 And they spake unto all the company of the children of Israel, saying, The land, which we passed through to search it, *is* an exceeding good land. If the LORD delight in us, then he will bring us into this land, and give it us; a land which floweth with milk and honey. Only rebel not ye against the LORD, neither fear ye the people of the land; for they *are* bread for us: their defence is departed from them, and the LORD *is* with us: fear them not.

There are some bold faith proclamations here:

- If the Lord is pleased with us, He will give us the land.
- Do not fear the people of the land, for they will be our prey.
- Their protection has been removed, and the Lord is with us!

These men did not deny the truth of the bad report; there were giants, fortified cities, and a strong army. But Joshua and Caleb focused on the Lord and His power. The other spies did the opposite and felt insignificant and incapable as a result. Being a prophetic church means that we live by every word that God speaks into our current situation, as it happens. We do not live on previous words, but proceeding ones. There is a revelatory rationale for all that God does. In transition, He is working to prepare us for the next dimension of life in the Spirit. There is a process to follow and understand. There is a breakthrough that comes with transition. Many churches do not survive the transition. They break up under the pressure.

Transition is the sternest test in a church's history. Only the best can take hold of their inheritance in the next stage. Beware the line of transition is not what we think it is! We realize the end of the transition stage long into the next stage.

Chapter Three
A New Church Arises In Revelation

I did a teaching series for over six hours and never came close to finishing all that God spoke. I am releasing an even more in depth writing in the next several Chapters of this book. Churches are in transition for a variety of reasons. Some are changing from being an excellent local church to having a resource church anointing.

This means an increase of vision and a new dimension of influence as more and more people are empowered and released. Some churches are becoming apostolic centers where the resident fivefold ministries enable the church to have an international significance in church planting and development. For many churches, though, transition will simply mean the process by which they embrace their corporate destiny at a much higher level.

Revelation is a level of transition you must go through in the building of the prototype Church. When the Lord seeks to move us into a new realm, He looks for us to have an increase of vision, anointing, and power.

There needs to come an increase of commitment and character. The process of transition always begins with revelation which is an insight from the Holy Spirit, possibly by prophetic disclosure. A prophetic word is released that inspires and ignites fresh faith regarding our destiny and overall vision as a church. The prophetic word may gather up previous words together with our current vision and take the whole concept much further forward. Revelation has impact. It will force us to re-examine where we are now and where we are going. Revelation brings appraisal and scrutiny to everything we have done and are currently doing. Revelation gets under our skin, making us feel excited about what is opening up to us in the future, but also apprehensive about what it all means. Revelation means change.

It is a beginning preceded by an ending, a closure and a new beginning, surrounded by vulnerability in the whole church. The prophetic word makes us feel great. We become excited by the vision but sobered by the change involved. Revelation may come by teaching. I have known several churches where new vision has arisen in the congregation because of teaching on the new church of the twenty-first century or new models of church. The members of that body have been caught up in faith to believe for and desire urgently to become such a church. The teaching has been a catalyst to create a different environment within which the members begin discussion and dialogue about structural changes, new vision, and a different spiritual culture.

I have known some churches where various people across the spiritual range of the work have had almost identical vision. The visions have been about moving to a new location, starting a new project, developing a range of new church initiatives, or a mixture of such actions. In several places, people had dreams that followed on and built up a picture of what God was revealing from one person to another.

What has been interesting in these events has been the diversity of people used by the Lord. The emotional makeup, character, and relationship between these people have been markedly different. That fact itself has given serious weight to the supernatural quality of the event. Of course, we do not change things based solely on dreams.

However, we do use them as a catalyst for prayer, discussion, and further seeking of the Lord. We can recognize that God has sovereignly intervened, and now we need to make ourselves available to the Holy Spirit and one another. Revelation also can come through apostolic insight and relationship. Many times there is an apostolic/prophetic visionary and a directive nature and quality to our discussions and relationship with our network friends and churches. We care and pray for one another. We stand together in times of tension and difficulty; we work side by side in the Kingdom, teaching, imparting, ministering to one another, and wanting the best for one another. These all act as a catalyst for fresh direction and insight into vision and destiny. Apostles can interpret events surrounding a church and give practical wisdom regarding a way forward.

We would expect revelation to flow out of these encounters, so that we can move forward with prayerful purpose. Revelation increases expectancy in the hearts of people, which is excellent and hopefully contagious, but it also creates problems for us in the outworkings of a new vision.

We want our people to be in faith and have confidence in the Lord. We want this new anticipation and excitement to touch as many as possible. But we must take care not to hype it up into something beyond what the Lord has spoken. Leaders often can go too far and turn anticipation into assumption in order to gather support for the new thing. If we can maintain a fair balance between excited vision and sober challenge, we will do well.

The only time we are completely balanced is when we stand still spiritually. Walking occurs when we throw our weight between one foot and another and maintain our momentum in a sense of direction. Spiritual balance is the movement of obedience and the distribution of faith between vision and sacrifice as we move together in unison. Expectancy can be dangerous for us if we are unfamiliar with how the Lord likes to work. Although vision and revelation combine to bring us a fresh sense of destiny, they also can inhibit our capacity for thoughtful preparation.

Luke 14:28-32 For which of you, intending to build a tower, sitteth not down first, and counteth the cost, whether he have *sufficient* to finish *it?* Lest haply, after he hath laid the foundation, and is not able to finish *it,* all that behold *it* begin to mock him, Saying, This man began to build, and was not able to finish. Or what king, going to make war against another king, sitteth not down first, and consulteth whether he be able with ten thousand to meet him that cometh against him with twenty thousand? Or else, while the other is yet a great way off, he sendeth an ambassage, and desireth conditions of peace.

We can get caught up in the excitement and go for it attitude, only to get caught out when something opposite happens. Hype invalidates reflection. Assumption derides consideration. Faith and caution are not in opposition. Faith wants to go for it! Caution wants to do it right. Faith says, "Yes! We're going to do it." Caution says, "This is how we should go about it." Caution brings strategy to the impetus of faith so that nothing is wasted. The main difference between the two is pace. Faith wants to get there immediately; caution wants to get there in one piece! Faith will pay the cost, whatever it is; caution does not want to pay more than necessary. Faith says, "Let's just pay it as we go." Caution says, "Let's budget for it before we start!" Caution and faith need one another. Without faith, caution will deliver a peacetime budget in a warfare situation. Without caution, faith will not have the strategy to overcome obstacles. Faith believes it can run a marathon and can't wait to start running. Caution knows how to run a marathon so that faith doesn't run out of steam. Faith plus caution is the marriage of particular knowledge and confident belief. Knowledge in this instance is the understanding of God's ways with a grasp of strategy and momentum. Everything has a rhythm in God. When He changes the momentum, the strategy must alter. Faith goes with the movement and momentum; caution goes with the rhythm and strategy.

The Lord will always make sure that every group has a mixture of these people within its membership. They are opposites in perception, but necessary allies in operation. This is the balance we must seek, the friendly interaction between faith and caution that allows us to run with patience the next stage of the great race. Faith is not mindless, nor caution faithless. They are the left and the right leg of movement. We need to understand them both and get them moving together if we are to avoid falling!

There is a reason for this partnership. Expectation on its own will speed up our momentum to the point of launching out into the atmosphere. We may be happy to boldly go where no church has gone before in our lifetime. Expectation searches out the horizon and seeks to get to the high point of anointing and power as quickly as possible.

In expectation, we are thinking horizon, but God is thinking about foundation. When revelation comes, we want to get there as quickly as possible. We are living by the prophetic power that captivates our hearts. However, there is a contradiction in the prophetic that declares to us, "You cannot get there from here." Contradiction is the journey from revelation to manifestation—the process of transition.

Joseph received a prophetic dream that he would one day have authority above his father and brothers.

Genesis 37:1-36 And Jacob dwelt in the land wherein his father was a stranger, in the land of Canaan. These *are* the generations of Jacob. Joseph, *being* seventeen years old, was feeding the flock with his brethren; and the lad *was* with the sons of Bilhah, and with the sons of Zilpah, his father's wives: and Joseph brought unto his father their evil report. Now Israel loved Joseph more than all his children, because he *was* the son of his old age: and he made him a coat of *many* colours. And when his brethren saw that their father loved him more than all his brethren, they hated him, and could not speak peaceably unto him. And Joseph dreamed a dream, and he told *it* his brethren: and they hated him yet the more. And he said unto them, Hear, I pray you, this dream which I have dreamed: For, behold, we *were* binding sheaves in the field, and, lo, my sheaf arose, and also stood upright; and, behold, your sheaves stood round about, and made obeisance to my sheaf. And his brethren said to him, Shalt thou indeed reign over us? or shalt thou indeed have dominion over us? And they hated him yet the more for his dreams, and for his words. And he dreamed yet another dream, and told it his brethren, and said, Behold, I have dreamed a dream more; and, behold, the sun and the moon and the eleven stars made obeisance to me. And he told *it* to his father, and to his brethren: and his father rebuked him, and said unto him, What *is* this dream that thou hast dreamed? Shall I and thy mother and thy brethren indeed come to bow down ourselves to thee to the earth? And his brethren envied him; but his father observed the saying. And his brethren went to feed their father's flock in Shechem. And Israel said unto Joseph, Do not thy brethren feed *the flock* in Shechem? come, and I will send thee unto them. And he said to him, Here *am I*. And he said to him, Go, I pray thee, see whether it be well with thy brethren, and well with the flocks; and bring me word again. So he sent him out of the vale of Hebron, and he came to Shechem. And a certain man found him, and, behold, *he was* wandering in the field: and the man asked him, saying, What seekest thou? And he said, I seek my brethren: tell me, I pray thee, where they feed *their flocks*. And the man said, They are departed hence; for I heard them say, Let us go to Dothan. And Joseph went after his brethren, and found them in Dothan. And when they saw him afar off, even before he came near unto them, they conspired against him to slay him. And they said one to another, Behold, this dreamer cometh. Come now therefore, and let us slay him, and cast him into some pit, and we will say, Some evil beast hath devoured him: and we shall see what will become of his dreams. And Reuben heard *it*, and he delivered him out of their hands; and said, Let us not kill him.

And Reuben said unto them, Shed no blood, *but* cast him into this pit that *is* in the wilderness, and lay no hand upon him; that he might rid him out of their hands, to deliver him to his father again. And it came to pass, when Joseph was come unto his brethren, that they stript Joseph out of his coat, *his* coat of *many* colours that *was* on him; And they took him, and cast him into a pit: and the pit *was* empty, *there was* no water in it. And they sat down to eat bread: and they lifted up their eyes and looked, and, behold, a company of Ishmeelites came from Gilead with their camels bearing spicery and balm and myrrh, going to carry *it* down to Egypt. And Judah said unto his brethren, What profit *is it* if we slay our brother, and conceal his blood? Come, and let us sell him to the Ishmeelites, and let not our hand be upon him; for he *is* our brother *and* our flesh. And his brethren were content. Then there passed by Midianites merchantmen; and they drew and lifted up Joseph out of the pit, and sold Joseph to the Ishmeelites for twenty *pieces* of silver: and they brought Joseph into Egypt. And Reuben returned unto the pit; and, behold, Joseph *was* not in the pit; and he rent his clothes. And he returned unto his brethren, and said, The child *is* not; and I, whither shall I go? And they took Joseph's coat, and killed a kid of the goats, and dipped the coat in the blood; And they sent the coat of *many* colours, and they brought *it* to their father; and said, This have we found: know now whether it *be* thy son's coat or no. And he knew it, and said, *It is* my son's coat; an evil beast hath devoured him; Joseph is without doubt rent in pieces. And Jacob rent his clothes, and put sackcloth upon his loins, and mourned for his son many days. And all his sons and all his daughters rose up to comfort him; but he refused to be comforted; and he said, For I will go down into the grave unto my son mourning. Thus his father wept for him. And the Midianites sold him into Egypt unto Potiphar, an officer of Pharaoh's, *and* captain of the guard.

The dream concerned them all bowing down to him. This prophecy was fulfilled eventually, but not before the opposite had occurred. After relating the dreams to his family, instead of them looking up at him, Joseph found himself in a pit looking up at them! He was sold as a slave and sent in chains to a distant country. His life had gone in the opposite direction to what he perhaps was expecting. Plainly, the Lord was not going to fulfill the prophecy over some empty-headed young man who did not have the sense to keep his mouth shut around some very irate brethren! After the calling comes the training. Once we have received serious prophetic input into our lives, we then need particular development before the word can be moved to a place of fulfillment. David found a similar set of circumstances at work in his own life. He was anointed to be king by the prophet Samuel. Nothing said or done at the time disclosed to David that he would be discredited and have to live in caves in the wilderness before the prophet's words came true.

Exodus 6:6-8 Wherefore say unto the children of Israel, I *am* the LORD, and I will bring you out from under the burdens of the Egyptians, and I will rid you out of their bondage, and I will redeem you with a stretched out arm, and with great judgments: And I will take you to me for a people, and I will be to you a God: and ye shall know that I *am* the LORD your God, which bringeth you out from under the burdens of the Egyptians. And I will bring you in unto the land, concerning the which I did swear to give it to Abraham, to Isaac, and to Jacob; and I will give it you for an heritage: I *am* the LORD.

The words never mentioned their journey into the wilderness or their subsequent testing by God as part of the means of fulfillment. This is the major part of the transitional and prophetic process. Before our destiny can be fulfilled, we must conform to all the character requirements that are a priority if we are to represent the God of Heaven. He wants all of us to conform to the image of Jesus as a prerequisite to fulfillment of prophecy. After the initial excitement of the word and the release of vision and destiny, God switches His attention to our character. Now He has to work on our personality, nature, and character, to elevate it to the point of approved trustworthiness. Our destiny is put on hold until the time that we are proved out in our character. After the prophecy, we are in the clouds with our destiny; however, the Lord is looking at something different! He is looking at our character and gauging the work and development we will need in order to develop us to that place of high calling.

This development will include a testing of our humility; our servant heart; our reliability under pressure; our truthfulness and purity; our leadership or ministry ability; our capacity to endure stress in warfare; our ability to learn from our mistakes; and above all, our conformity to His love, grace, mercy, and kindness. All these will come under intense scrutiny in the most difficult and trying of circumstances. It is almost as though, at the same time as we are still day-dreaming after the prophetic word, the Lord trips us up, throws us into a dark room, and beats the living daylights out of us! At least, that is what it feels like. Our lives run in the opposite direction for a time as God begins to work with our character. It is here that most people let go of their vision and call.

The instinctive reaction for many people, when their lives begin to run in conflicting directions to their prophecy, is to blame the prophet. It is easy to assume that because the prophet said one thing and the opposite is now occurring, then the prophecy is false. However, most accusations of false prophecy in this instance are made because of ignorance about process. Process is a journey, a series of stages between one dimension and another. The journey is not in a straight line of upward development from the point of origin.

The process of God in developing our potential into something actual involves the releasing of revelation. This causes us to look up to determine our destiny, but it is followed by a decline in our fortunes as we plunge into confrontation in transition.

Chapter Four
A New Church Arises In Confrontation

Revelation leads us to a point of confrontation. You must understand we must experience all levels of transition. Literally everything within our church that would prevent God from fulfilling His word to us will be examined. The bottom will seem like it is falling out from under the church. We will feel ourselves dropping into our own version of Joseph's pit. Before we receive the power of His resurrection, we must experience something of the fellowship of His sufferings. Before the release of His life, there is conformity to His death. Paul said that death works in us so that life could work in others.

2 Corinthians 4:12 So then death worketh in us, but life in you.

If we want to know Him in resurrection power, then we have to know Him in the fellowship of His suffering, because the two things are combined. If God has promised us life, He will give us death first, because death works life in us. We have to understand the mind of God and the ways of God. God will always deliver us to death.

2 Corinthians 4:11 For we which live are alway delivered unto death for Jesus' sake, that the life also of Jesus might be made manifest in our mortal flesh.

When Jesus was on the cross, He said, "It is finished," but He didn't ascend directly into Heaven from that point; He descended into hell. It was from hell that He went up to being seated at the right hand of the Father. Even for Jesus, that point of "It is finished" was not the end of His ordeal. What He meant was that one part was finished, but now He had another part to accomplish. He had to take back the keys and confound the enemy. He went down before He went up. He went down into hell for a purpose: to lead captivity captive, to render the enemy powerless, to take the keys of the kingdom, and to conquer death and hell.

This part on earth was finished, but the part in the spiritual realm was not finished. So He had to go down before He could go up, and we will find that the same is true for us. There are key things that have to happen in this period of confrontation. If we do not submit to God in the confrontational period, we will not experience the transformation that needs to happen so that we can occupy what God has promised. The next thing that will happen at some point is that all hell will break loose from inside the church. We will find that instead of climbing into a spiritual dimension, we will drop into a carnal one. We will find levels of immaturity that we did not believe could exist amongst senior Christians in our midst.

We will find childishness, irritability, flesh, strife, envy, and hunger for position, as the pride and ambition of people begin to surface. As the destiny of the church begins to unfold, instead of realizing our potential for greatness, we must come to terms with our capacity for carnal behavior. God gets to work on our flesh and, instead of being elevated to a new place in the spirit, we plunge into carnality. Why? Because God is determined to get rid of everything in us that is rotten. We will be plunged as a church into a period of confrontation. The enemy will attack the vision and the leadership. There will be criticism and resentment. Old power struggles will resurface and old wounds will be re-opened. Anything inside us that is unresolved will come to the surface, because that is the whole point of confrontation.

We can get into the place where God wants us to be only when we actually go by way of the cross. God will take us right to that. He won't take us up into the heights; He will take us down into the depths. We will go into the grave and God will deal with our flesh life. The enemy will be active all around the church, but we need to know that God is going to use him to get rid of the flesh. The blessing of God may continue to fall because the Lord will not leave us comfortless. This continued blessing is the goodness of God at work. God is simultaneous in His actions; that is, He is always doing several things at once in our lives. These actions do not have to add up together. They can be all separate and not necessarily linked in any way. We all have known God's blessing on our lives; even as at the same time, the Holy Spirit convicts us of personal sin. Similarly, we have experienced the power of God corporately despite internal carnality and lack of unity.

When farmers plow their fields and then level them for planting, we see a wonderful flat surface waiting for new seed. If there is a rainfall on that field, though, the next day it will be covered in stones. The rain softens the ground, allowing what is hard within it to come to the surface. In a similar way, anything that is hard in our lives will come to the surface in this time of confrontation. If this is happening now in the church where you are serving, take heart. God is getting rid of the flesh; the vision has not gone away and the prophecy was not wrong. God has the vision safe. It will be restored to you after the process is complete, provided that you obey and submit to Him in transition. Give Him what He wants. In transition, we are in the process of God making us fit the word He gave us. We may feel that we are moving further and further away from the revelation that God gave us. This is no time to look at our destiny. We must behold the process and begin to look at the character of the church. This is not a time to dwell on projects, begin new initiatives, or commit ourselves to new ventures of faith.

If we are in confrontation, it is because God is dealing with something that should not be there. Depending on where the church is in the process, we do not know how many people will leave the work during this period of testing. Most churches going through transition will suffer a contraction in their resources. Finances, personnel, key people in ministry, and leadership may flow out of the church initially. Some will be friends leaving us for other pastures when the going gets tough. Generally, these people may be no significant loss. We cannot lose people who were never with us in heart in the first place. Others may be more key to our progress, and losing them will hurt us. Some will go because they may move with a job change. If things were different, they may have refused the promotion or change of work situation, but now they feel it necessary to pursue church elsewhere. Some will leave to start a new work locally and may try to take others with them. God will always reduce us to that which is precious. Of course, for some it is the right time to go because the Lord does have other plans. Generally, though, when the heat is fierce, we are burning up that which is wood, hay, and stubble.

1 Corinthians 3:12-15 Now if any man build upon this foundation gold, silver, precious stones, wood, hay, stubble; Every man's work shall be made manifest: for the day shall declare it, because it shall be revealed by fire; and the fire shall try every man's work of what sort it is. If any man's work abide which he hath built thereupon, he shall receive a reward. If any man's work shall be burned, he shall suffer loss: but he himself shall be saved; yet so as by fire.

After the process, we may have a church that is leaner by number, but fitter in spirit. The gifts and the calling of God are without repentance. Let God hold on to the vision and the future; we must hold on to Him and one another. It is the age-old battle of the Spirit against the flesh.

There are some attitudes, mind-sets, and approaches that simply have to change. In confrontation, the Lord will touch our selfishness, self-preoccupation, and self-centered behavior. We all will be humbled in some way before God is satisfied that He can release us to the next level of anointing.

It seems a contradiction, but it is true, that the prophetic word about expansion should cause us to enter a period of contraction. Our first stop on the confrontation process is the cross of Jesus, followed by the grave. Death must work in our midst to God's satisfaction. In this process, we discover that both God and the devil have their own agenda. God's agenda is life, the realization of the vision, and the entrance into a deeper anointing and a more powerful spiritual dimension. The devil's agenda is the destruction of all that we hold dear at this present time.

1 Peter 5:8-10 Be sober, be vigilant; because your adversary the devil, as a roaring lion, walketh about, seeking whom he may devour: Whom resist stedfast in the faith, knowing that the same afflictions are accomplished in your brethren that are in the world. But the God of all grace, who hath called us unto his eternal glory by Christ Jesus, after that ye have suffered a while, make you perfect, stablish, strengthen, settle *you*.

We are encountering nothing new; we are dealing with nothing that has not been the experience of countless churches. Out of this period of suffering will come the approval of God to take us on into His plan and purpose. The enemy has three strategies in mind to use against us in this period of difficulty.

The problem with confrontation is often the timing in which it occurs. No time seems to be the right time, but some are more problematic than others. It is very difficult when our church is going through this painful process of transition, whereas churches around us are enjoying a laughing anointing! We are going through our worst time ever as a church while others are basking in renewal. The most natural thing to do at a time like this is to look for something at fault and someone to blame.

If we have no revelatory rationale for current events, we will interpret them from the soul rather than from the spirit man. Instead of looking beyond the circumstances to detect the fine hand of God at work, people look for the obvious and interpret it according to their own thinking and feeling. If the facts themselves are not obvious or do not add up totally to cover the difficulty, we invent things from our imagination, supplying spiritual reasoning to our own particular actions. It is always incredibly difficult to see other churches being blessed when we are under trial and testing. People would rather believe that there is a problem in the leadership; there is sin in the camp; that we have the wrong vision; or that we are out of the will of God. They do not understand the purposes of God. The same process will come to every church in some way as God cleanses the temple of the Church. When something bad happens, it is easier to believe that it is the devil's work.

It may well be true, but we do need the perspective of the Holy Spirit in order to see where the hand of God is moving.

He allows in His wisdom what He could easily prevent by His power! God is dealing with our flesh and our capacity to be carnal. The flesh is the only means whereby satan can get his hooks into the church. The flesh is a bigger problem to the church than any demonic intervention. The enemy tends to overplay his hand and his work becomes obvious. The flesh is much more insidious. It has many disguises and hiding places and can flare up in the most surprising of people. Many churches are not yet good enough to be attacked by direct demonic activity. Their flesh is too good of a target to miss. Why assign a demon power to disrupt the church when pushing a few flesh buttons will have a similar effect? We do an excellent job ourselves in terms of disruption and division, when we allow the flesh-life to remain unchecked and not accountable. Confrontation is the process by which God begins to work on our character and our lifestyle.

John 14:30 Hereafter I will not talk much with you: for the prince of this world cometh, and hath nothing in me.

Confrontation is designed to remove every hook of the flesh in our lives. The Lord will plunge us into crisis where every shameful thing hidden behind our public mask of spirituality will begin to surface. When the Spirit falls, the flesh will always rise. These two are ancient enemies who cannot abide each other's company. Confrontation is the internal battle for spiritual supremacy. Will we see the carnal man crowned as the overriding power of our lives, or will the humility, gentleness, and meekness of Christ be fashioned within us as we submit to the Holy Spirit? Will we stand and be faithful to God and people around us, or will we quit and move on, perhaps to repeat the cycle elsewhere? Of course, not all such outward/onward movements are wrong; there are many new alignments taking place in these days as the Lord repositions His people for growth. Confrontation is God attacking the flesh. It is the work of the cross in our hearts. It is about laying down personal agendas and realizing that the Lord is killing our pride, ambition, and lack of real servanthood. He is dealing with our sin nature and our sin habit. He is breaking us; crushing us in the winepress of His dealings; chastising and scourging our carnal behavior; and getting rid of the enmity within us that casts a shadow over our relationships with Christ and His Body.

Throughout all these trials and difficulties, the Lord uses confrontation to make us fit and ready for all that He has planned. Many churches will not graduate to the real battlefield. They are still in spiritual kindergarten because the flesh has not been laid to rest. God has to deal with the enemy within before He can lead us to conquer the enemy on any external battleground. In infiltration, the enemy seeks to get between people, to penetrate relationships with his poison. Marriages are a favorite target. It is hard to concentrate on spiritual developments in the church when our home-life is a battlefield of emotional hurts. Leadership teams are a choice target.

There is a simple strategy at work here: If the head is damaged, the body is made powerless. Any relationship of note and significance will come under attack in this scheme of infiltration. The devil will use ambition in people to divide and rule. He will create power struggles in key people. Unresolved issues will be encouraged to flare up again; grudges will get another opportunity to express themselves; unforgiveness will manifest itself in some pseudo-spiritual manner. Long-standing resentments, roots of bitterness, and hidden agendas will all surface at this time. The enemy will use any ego that is unbroken, any unredeemed personality or character trait to accomplish his design. All of it will be respectfully hidden under a covering, under a veneer of spirituality. These are all points of entry where the flesh cannot resist the touch of the devil.

1 Corinthians 1:10-13 Now I beseech you, brethren, by the name of our Lord Jesus Christ, that ye all speak the same thing, and *that* there be no divisions among you; but *that* ye be perfectly joined together in the same mind and in the same judgment. For it hath been declared unto me of you, my brethren, by them *which are of the house* of Chloe, that there are contentions among you. Now this I say, that every one of you saith, I am of Paul; and I of Apollos; and I of Cephas; and I of Christ. Is Christ divided? was Paul crucified for you? or were ye baptized in the name of Paul?

1 Corinthians 3:1-9 And I, brethren, could not speak unto you as unto spiritual, but as unto carnal, *even* as unto babes in Christ. I have fed you with milk, and not with meat: for hitherto ye were not able *to bear it,* neither yet now are ye able. For ye are yet carnal: for whereas *there is* among you envying, and strife, and divisions, are ye not carnal, and walk as men? For while one saith, I am of Paul; and another, I *am* of Apollos; are ye not carnal? Who then is Paul, and who *is* Apollos, but ministers by whom ye believed, even as the Lord gave to every man? I have planted, Apollos watered; but God gave the increase. So then neither is he that planteth any thing, neither he that watereth; but God that giveth the increase. Now he that planteth and he that watereth are one: and every man shall receive his own reward according to his own labour. For we are labourers together with God: ye are God's husbandry, *ye are* God's building.

The more spiritual the devil can make the flesh appear, the less likely we are to understand that we have been infiltrated. In the Corinthian church, divisiveness was revealing itself in the fake spiritual dialogue of the flesh playing "follow my leader". Paul wisely cut through all this nonsense to expose carnal behavior on all sides. Carnality inhibits revelation. It keeps us in spiritual infancy where we are unable to be trusted with real truth and power.

1 Corinthians 11:17-19 Now in this that I declare *unto you* I praise *you* not, that ye come together not for the better, but for the worse. For first of all, when ye come together in the church, I hear that there be divisions among you; and I partly believe it. For there must be also heresies among you, that they which are approved may be made manifest among you.

Handling the potential for division is a major part of growing up as a church. God does not create this scenario, but He does allow it to happen for a purpose. God allows power struggles so that the church can identify who are the real leaders. In the time of conflict and power struggle, we find which leaders are really concerned about the flock and which people are more concerned about their own status and position. We discover, beneath all the spiritual language, who are preoccupied with their own vision, ministry, and anointing. People in the church are frightened of division. They will offer any compromise between factions in order to keep things together in some appearance of unity. The issue here is not unity; it is approval. On whom is the hand of the Lord resting for focal leadership? To be able to discern correctly, examine the behavior of the people involved. Is there someone who is being domineering, controlling, or manipulative? Is there somebody behind the scenes behaving dishonorably? Is there somebody walking around getting into every house telling stories? Is there someone on the phone to everybody causing divisions and divisiveness? Who is doing the peaceful thing, and who is doing the troublesome thing?

In that way, the church will know who is approved of God, because those who behave righteously in a situation are approved, while those who behave unrighteously are not. Why? Because they are grabbing for power themselves. That is where the church has to learn wisdom. Times of divisiveness are actually very important in determining who are the real "called of God" leadership in this body of people. Do not be afraid of the potential for division; just look to see how people are operating.

Those who behave righteously in accordance with the fruit of the Spirit and the character of God are approved; those who are doing the opposite are clearly not, because they are walking in the flesh to get their own way. It is part of God's way of shaping us for war so that when we get on the real battlefield, we can be confident that the person leading us has the approval and mandate of the Lord. This person really cares for our soul and will not leave us when the going gets tough. We know that we have a captain at the church and not a corporal with delusions of splendor. Most people with some semblance of anointing can usually talk the talk, but actions under stress reveal character. Infiltration is about the enemy gaining a point of entry to get power in the church, which will lead him to his next part of the strategy.

Continuous attack upon and within the leadership has a devastating effect upon the soul as well as on the effectiveness of the church. Internal strife leads to a depression of faith, low self-esteem in prayer, and dispirited worship. The enemy wants to cause as much pain as possible so that the church will be unable to carry on in its current form. The more strife he can generate at this point, the stronger a hold he has on the church both now and in the future. Even if the issues are resolved and we stay together, he is hoping that enough damage will have occurred relationally to make the possibility of further infiltration more likely. He is quite happy for us to resolve our issues as long as there is uneasiness in our hearts toward one another and the pain of the circumstances we have endured has not been healed. This gives him ammunition for another day. This is important to understand. We must not have resolution at any cost. To compromise now is only to store up problems for later. Christians are famous for sweeping things under the carpet. We must insist on forgiveness, inner healing, and true restoration of relationships as a prerequisite for moving forward together.

The activity, program, and vision of the church must be put on hold for a season in order for full restoration to be made. Otherwise, action will dilute reconciliation. This will leave gaps for the enemy to exploit at a later date. The internal war must be fully won before the real external conflict can begin. I do not want to go into real extended conflict with the enemy if people on my side are still holding grievances. The purpose of depression is to demoralize. It is to create as much pain, hardship, woundedness, and resentment as possible; it is to paralyze the leadership into inactivity. Depression prevents active faith by setting people against one another, so that everyone becomes weary and lethargic. Its purpose is to bring the church to a place of battle fatigue and exhaustion. Under depression, the flesh regurgitates history. We go back over the old ground we thought had been dealt with already. The enemy digs up the store of ammunition that he buried the last time we had an internal conflict. Unresolved issues sweep through our emotions, creating further hopelessness and sadness. When past history is raised, our current confusion is deepened. That is why we cannot move on from our current crisis without real forgiveness and restoration. Where there has been a breakdown of love, trust, unity, and peace in relationships, real restoration must take place. Otherwise, we just bury our emotions for the enemy to exhume later. Any promotion of disloyalty, betrayal, and unfaithfulness must be thoroughly cleansed. All behind-the-scenes sniping and negative fellowship must be fully repented of before we can move forward, or we will simply revert when the pressure returns.

If we care more about what we each think, feel, and want than we do about relationships in the church, we must beware! We badly need to examine ourselves before the Lord, because we are more liable to be part of the problem than the answer. At this point, infiltration has occurred and depression has set in, pushing us away from one another and therefore away from the purpose of God. Any cliques that form will have more potential for divisiveness than unity, even if our motives are honorable. It is simply too easy to become negative even in a wholesome way in these circumstances. All of us must be very, very careful before the Lord.

Things said and done now will have repercussions for years. Godly conduct and honorable behavior will enable us to reap the blessing of God for years to come. But disgraceful behavior will sow discord, continuously resulting in constant reoccurrence of internal fleshly conflict. Even meeting together in small groups for prayer can be fraught with hidden negativity. Emotions and thoughts in times of stress demand expression. We can find ourselves talking about the issues for two hours and praying for 15 minutes. Sarcastically, it is churches that have successfully negotiated these turbulent waters that have formulated core values and principles of behavior. Our God is a God of principle. His nature is unchanging, no matter what occurs. He has core values from which He operates that provide radiant confidence to all who know Him and walk with Him.

Hebrews 13:8 Jesus Christ the same yesterday, and to day, and for ever.

Core values represent the unchanging personality of God and are what we fall back on in times of relational conflict. Debilitating depression is what occurs when we have not properly defined our core values. We therefore will react to people and situations rather than respond to the Lord. Core values enable us to focus on God and be led by the Spirit. We do not become mixed up in the carnality; rather, we allow our response to elevate us into the nature and character of God. So we practice peacemaking, love, gentleness, self-control, and kindness. Depression causes isolation. People leave the church in search of blessing and new beginnings.

The purpose of confrontation is to create a spiritual transformation within our lives, enabling us to grow up and put on the new nature. Leaving in search of blessing may seem desirable at the time, but mostly we only confirm our immaturity and inability to move up to the next level of anointing. When spiritual depression takes hold, we are ripe for the final scheme of the devil's strategy. Obedience is interesting to note that the people who tend to suffer the most in internal strife are the wives and children of leaders in the church. Most leaders are used to stress, conflict, and spiritual attack. It is their family who will come under the most direct attack. Wives in particular seem to take the brunt of relational conflict.

The number of people they can talk to and confide in is at best drastically reduced if not completely destroyed. They have to be more careful than anyone else in case an unguarded word spoken in confidence is repeated by a friend who means well but acts thoughtlessly. This is just one of the many reasons why the church must agree on an external individual or group to come and help them through the crisis. We need objectivity and a wider perspective on what God is doing. We need help to be both reconciled and restored. We need to determine our core values. External friendship and support that is impartial and anointed can enable us to emerge with credit, integrity, and destiny intact. The team helping us through must firstly focus on character and the fruit of the Spirit before we get into the debate. Each of us must learn how to focus on our integrity, Christlikeness, and morality before we can realistically begin to debate the issues. What type of behavior does God expect of us in these circumstances? Secondly, the team must release revelation into the church regarding the purpose of God at this time, so that we all are clear about what the Lord wants to achieve in this crisis. They must reveal the process behind the crisis so that we have a path to follow. This will lessen many unnecessary words and feelings as we deal with them personally at the source. Thirdly, any outstanding grievances and judgments from a previous time must be dealt with now as a priority. We must spike the enemy ammunition and render it useless. We need a declared amnesty so that old issues can be laid to rest and not become part of the current situation. Finally, they must be allowed to arbitrate the issues to a meaningful and long-lasting settlement, at the heart of which is genuine reconciliation of relationships and restoration of vision and purpose.

It is important that this external team has the broad support of the majority of the people and that they are truly capable of being objective and impartial. This is not Christian gang activity where we get our friends in to get others to toe the line! Without that external frame of reference, we will slide quickly into depression and passivity. If the crisis goes on too long without resolution, some will give up. A depression will set in that hinders prayer and productivity. Some will cease trying to participate. Lateness or non-attendance in meetings will become prevalent. There will be no spark in worship because emotions are at a low level. Some will be hoping that a word of faith may penetrate the fog of their uncertainty. We will have lost our ability to generate faith from within our own spirit. We will become tired and dispirited, too weary even to continue talking over the same ground. We will have no energy. Everything will be a trial and a pain. We will sadly conclude that it is better for us to leave. We may search for spiritual reasons regarding why we are jumping ship more to make ourselves feel better than to validate our actions. Some will simply fold their tents and steal away. Our ability to focus on anything significant will be much reduced. We will feel isolated and unsure of who we can properly relate to in the church. There will be a loss of faith and initiative. Subversion and passivity will become the order of the day. Faithfulness will be discontinued by some people, particularly in the area of personal help and financial support. Key workers will lose their drive and take sabbaticals. Financial input will drop as people withhold their substance until the situation stabilizes. Unfortunately, many of these people do not store up their tithes and offerings; they just stop giving! Some will begin to choose sides in the issue or try to stay neutral. We will choose sides often on the basis of friendship rather than obedience to God or any outward signs of righteousness and morality. We will not imagine that it is possible for people to be right about the issue but morally corrupt in their behavior and how they handle the situation.

I have known men to be very accurate about the issues but use the situation to feed their own selfish desires and ambition. I also have known people who have been wrong about the issue but morally cautious in how they handled the situation. Character under stress is more valuable than an accurate diagnosis. In situations containing great potential for unrighteous behavior, always mark the people who behave like Jesus. Obedience is destructive and will lead to division and a continuance of improper behavior, resulting in ongoing strife within the village, town, city, or region.

Even the people who left the church early on in the dispute will still snipe at people from the cowardly safety of noninvolvement. There may be another column still at work within the body perpetuating the infiltration, depression, and ongoing passivity that the enemy so loves. Those who left will still want their influence to be felt in the work. They will not be under authority anymore, but they will still persist in sowing their perspective however relevant or poisonous it may be into the homes of people who have chosen to stay.

This type of activity could probably fall into the category of manipulation, control, and domination. We must abandon our place in the issue. We have no voice now and must render our part in the issue inactive. If we are sought out, we must express no opinion. It is important to be thoroughly correct in our thinking, speaking, and behaving. We can pray blessing on people but must not give advice. If we have taken ourselves out, we must stay out! The wrath of God at this type of behavior will eventually catch up with us later as we reap whatever we sow. I have known many churches to begin operation in times like this and suffer the exact same reversal. When churches are going through internal strife, it is my practice to determine the source of their beginning.

If God does not own the getting of something, He cannot own the having of it! How we start dictates how we finish. Churches that began in rebellion will end in humiliation. We must determine the reason for our current distress in the church and not just assume we are in transition to a more powerful place.

Is He scourging us of our arrogance and ambition? Must we make an act of public repentance and contrition in order to set right the past and bring healing and reconciliation? If so, we need to appoint an external team to help us fully obey the process of repentance. However, it simply may be that the Lord never intended our church to start. He was never in the split and does not endorse our activity. We may have blessed people individually (because God is faithful to us personally), but we have never been able to grow corporately to any level of significance. Our corporate vision has never taken off; we have found ourselves stumbling from one good idea to another, but nothing has really worked. We have a modicum of success but no sustainable breakthrough. People join and people leave, but spiritually we are not really going anywhere. Our church may have a history of continuous divisiveness and splitting. That may tell us something if we have the heart to listen. We may well be wasting our life and our substance on something that will never grow from personal blessing into corporate anointing. In crisis, we must evaluate our history in an attitude of openness and honesty. We can fool ourselves and deceive other people, but God is not mocked. What we sow, we will reap. Some churches need to close their doors and disband. Whatever spirit of division and rebellion that we have entertained and given room to; must be driven out of the area. We must apologize to other churches. Our people must be delivered of rebellion and deception before being placed honorably with other churches. Any revenue from the sale of property and equipment plus the current account can be given to missions or sowed into the unity of the churches in the area. What began in dishonor can be terminated in full righteousness, giving no place to the enemy. Our demise must be honorable, or we sow continuous problems into other churches through the conduct of the people we have given away. Receiving churches must be kind and merciful but firm enough in relationship to ensure that past behavior does not remain current practice.

Confrontation is the touch of God against the flesh. It is the hand of God moving unseen behind the enemy and sinful man, orchestrating the downfall of everything that would prevent Him from achieving His dream for the church. The Lord uses everything to destroy the work of the world, the flesh, and devil in our midst. However, it is not all gloom and doom. In the midst of the desperate process of change, we will see the Christ walking among us spreading His fragrance and beauty in our hearts. Heaven will come to earth as the Holy Spirit broods over our seeming chaos, affecting a transforming work in our lives. We will suffer the loss of many things, but we will gain the one thing that makes it all worthwhile: the love of Jesus...the beauty of His presence manifested among us.

Continuous attack upon and within the leadership has a devastating effect upon the soul as well as on the effectiveness of the church. Internal strife leads to a depression of faith, low self-esteem in prayer, and dispirited worship. The enemy wants to cause as much pain as possible so that the church will be unable to carry on in its current form. The more strife he can generate at this point, the stronger a hold he has on the church both now and in the future. Even if the issues are resolved and we stay together, he is hoping that enough damage will have occurred relationally to make the possibility of further infiltration more likely. He is quite happy for us to resolve our issues as long as there is uneasiness in our hearts toward one another and the pain of the circumstances we have endured has not been healed. This gives him ammunition for another day. This is important to understand. We must not have resolution at any cost. To compromise now is only to store up problems for later. Christians are famous for sweeping things under the carpet. We must insist on forgiveness, inner healing, and true restoration of relationships as a prerequisite for moving forward together. The activity, program, and vision of the church must be put on hold for a season in order for full restoration to be made. Otherwise, action will dilute reconciliation. This will leave gaps for the enemy to exploit at a later date. The internal war must be fully won before the real external conflict can begin.

I do not want to go into real extended conflict with the enemy if people on my side are still holding grievances. The purpose of depression is to demoralize. It is to create as much pain, hardship, woundedness, and resentment as possible; it is to paralyze the leadership into inactivity. Depression prevents active faith by setting people against one another, so that everyone becomes weary and sluggish. Its purpose is to bring the church to a place of battle fatigue and exhaustion. Under depression, the flesh regurgitates history. We go back over the old ground we thought had been dealt with already. The enemy digs up the store of ammunition that he buried the last time we had an internal conflict. Unresolved issues sweep through our emotions, creating further hopelessness and sadness. When past history is raised, our current confusion is deepened. That is why we cannot move on from our current crisis without real forgiveness and restoration.

Where there has been a breakdown of love, trust, unity, and peace in relationships, real restoration must take place. Otherwise, we just bury our emotions for the enemy to exhume later. Any promotion of disloyalty, betrayal, and unfaithfulness must be thoroughly cleansed. All behind-the-scenes sniping and negative fellowship must be fully repented of before we can move forward, or we will simply revert when the pressure returns. If we care more about what we each think, feel, and want than we do about relationships in the church, we must beware! We badly need to examine ourselves before the Lord, because we are more liable to be part of the problem than the answer. At this point, infiltration has occurred and depression has set in, pushing us away from one another and therefore away from the purpose of God. Any cliques that form will have more potential for divisiveness than unity, even if our motives are honorable. It is simply too easy to become negative even in a wholesome way in these circumstances. All of us must be very, very careful before the Lord. Things said and done now will have repercussions for years. Godly conduct and honorable behavior will enable us to reap the blessing of God for years to come. But disgraceful behavior will sow discord, continuously resulting in constant re-occurrence of internal fleshly conflict.

Even meeting together in small groups for prayer can be full with hidden negativity. Emotions and thoughts in times of stress demand expression. We can find ourselves talking about the issues for two hours and praying for 15 minutes. Sarcastically, it is churches that have successfully negotiated these turbulent waters that have formulated core values and principles of behavior. Our God is a God of principle. His nature is unchanging, no matter what occurs. He has core values from which He operates that provide radiant confidence to all who know Him and walk with Him.

Core values represent the unchanging personality of God and are what we fall back on in times of relational conflict. Debilitating depression is what occurs when we have not properly defined our core values. We therefore will react to people and situations rather than respond to the Lord. Core values enable us to focus on God and be led by the Spirit. We do not become mixed up in the carnality; rather, we allow our response to elevate us into the nature and character of God. So we practice peacemaking, love, gentleness, self-control, and kindness. Depression causes isolation. People leave the church in search of blessing and new beginnings. The purpose of confrontation is to create a spiritual transformation within our lives, enabling us to grow up and put on the new nature.

The number of people they can talk to and confide in is at best drastically reduced if not completely destroyed. They have to be more careful than anyone else in case an unguarded word spoken in confidence is repeated by a friend who means well but acts thoughtlessly. This is just one of the many reasons why the church must agree on an external individual or group to come and help them through the crisis. We need objectivity and a wider perspective on what God is doing. We need help to be both reconciled and restored. We need to determine our core values. External friendship and support that is impartial and anointed can enable us to emerge with credit, integrity, and destiny intact. The team helping us through must firstly focus on character and the fruit of the Spirit before we get into the debate. Each of us must learn how to focus on our integrity, Christlikeness, and morality before we can realistically begin to debate the issues. What type of behavior does God expect of us in these circumstances?

Chapter Five
A New Church Arises In Transformation

One of the major parts of transition is the part of transforming into who God has called you to be. Through the violence of the confrontational issues surrounding us, God does a work of transformation. In the stormy process of spirit versus flesh, He removes our old nature and soaks us in the new nature of Christ

As we submit to the will of God, we learn obedience through our suffering and deliver ourselves to a place where God can trust us.

Nehemiah 8:10 Then he said unto them, Go your way, eat the fat, and drink the sweet, and send portions unto them for whom nothing is prepared: for *this* day *is* holy unto our Lord: neither be ye sorry; for the joy of the LORD is your strength.

For the joy set before us, we can endure this divine treatment of the cross in our lives. As we learn to humble ourselves, the Father will joyfully fill us with a greater presence of His Son.

As the manifestation of Christ's presence increases, so does the fruit of the Spirit; this is the nature of God. Our pleasure in God increases and we are filled with joy, encouragement, and comfort of the Spirit. Our desire for the Lord increases with our submission, turning to delight in our daily lives. Confrontation/transformation is a combined process engineered by God to kill off our flesh and enliven us in His Spirit. Unless we allow ourselves to submit to the Lord, we can never fully inherit the totality of our prophetic call.

The process worked in Joseph but failed in Saul, where David's life appears to be a cycle of contradiction that constantly brought him into confrontation with God and transformation within. God eventually regretted making Saul king because it seemed that he could never grasp the significance of the process the Lord was using to change him.

Acts 13:22 And when he had removed him, he raised up unto them David to be their king; to whom also he gave testimony, and said, I have found David the *son* of Jesse, a man after mine own heart, which shall fulfil all my will.

When Israel came out of Egypt, the shortest route to Canaan was through Philistine territory. Though Israel was armed for battle, the Lord took the people the long way round because they were not ready for the fight.

Exodus 13:17 And it came to pass, when Pharaoh had let the people go, that God led them not *through* the way of the land of the Philistines, although that *was* near; for God said, Lest peradventure the people repent when they see war, and they return to Egypt:

There are shortcuts in the Spirit, but you have to be of a certain caliber and quality to endure the fight that you will find on that journey. It is not easy! The desert route was God's way of changing weaklings into warriors. The church is looking for acts of power to provide a shortcut into a new dimension of life, love, and service. However, every move of God delivers us to the cross of Christ, from which there is no escape. The move of God within us creates a willingness to take up the cross, die daily, and follow Jesus. The cross understands the process of death to life that the Lord is establishing in our lives. In the process of transformation, God has three strategies to combat the schemes of the devil and to establish His own will in the church. It is confrontation for a season to provide transformation for a reason. In order to occupy the high territory of the Spirit that is our inheritance, we must conform to the image of Christ and become supernatural as Christ is formed within.

Hebrews 12:2 Looking unto Jesus the author and finisher of *our* faith; who for the joy that was set before him endured the cross, despising the shame, and is set down at the right hand of the throne of God.

This must become our response also in this direct work of the cross. God is nailing things in our lives that simply must die. It pleased God to bruise Jesus, and it pleases God to bruise us also. It is supposed to be painful. However, in transformation, we also will know incredible love and comfort as God soothes our pain and ministers to us in our distress.

In the Garden of Gethsemane, an angel ministered to Jesus as He prayed to be wholehearted in the will of God, knowing the suffering that would entail.

Luke 22:43 And there appeared an angel unto him from heaven, strengthening him.

God is bringing us to a place where He can actually trust us with the very thing that He prophesied over us in the first place. He is doing a work of transformation. He is purifying the temple, cleaning His house. He is pruning us, cutting us back that we might become more fruitful. We can consciously work toward His goal or unconsciously oppose it. If we cooperate, it is a short, sharp, intense, and very painful death. If we resist or fail to flow with the process of change, we unwittingly make the whole thing longer than perhaps necessary.

The reason that confrontation and transformation are combined into one process is because God wants us to behold Jesus. He wants us to hold on to Him and be held by Him. We do not enter and endure contradiction and then pass through transformation. If they followed after each other, none of us would make it. They are a combined work of God. The devil is loose, but Jesus is present! The flesh is dying but the new nature is rising. We are losing our friends in the natural but growing in friendship with God in the Spirit. We are shedding our old wineskin and forming a new one. The first of God's three strategies is communion with Him. God wants to be present as we transition. How do we enter into communion with God? The first thing we have to do is humble ourselves before God.

If we humble ourselves, He will exalt us in due time. If we exalt ourselves by not giving in to the process, it will be harder for us later on. The more you keep running away, the more difficult you are going to make it for yourself. God is going to get more and more difficult with you. Jesus put it this way: You can either stumble over this rock and be broken, or this rock can fall on you and you will be crushed. I would rather be broken than crushed, but I cannot avoid being hit. I want to stumble over this thing and be broken. I do not want something to fall on me from a great height and crush me. You pay your money and make your choice, and my choice is to stay here and die right now. I want to be more conscious of the glory of change in transformation than I am of the pain of change in confrontation. I want communion with God, so I am prepared to humble myself so that I can please Him with all my responses. On the days when I have to grit my teeth, cry my tears, and endure, I want to hold on to Him as He holds on to me. On the days when I can smile because the pain is just a dull ache, I want to resolve to continue with God in the process.

James 5:10, 11 Take, my brethren, the prophets, who have spoken in the name of the Lord, for an example of suffering affliction, and of patience. Behold, we count them happy which endure. Ye have heard of the patience of Job, and have seen the end of the Lord; that the Lord is very pitiful, and of tender mercy.

If we really are going to rise to a place where our own personal anointing and faith level is high, then we are going to need to know what real communion with God is. All ministries come out of relationship. Power comes out of suffering, and anointing comes out of intimacy. It is in communion with God that we learn how to humble ourselves under His hand. There is no point in complaining. The most positive thing we can do in confrontation is to fast and humble ourselves before God. We then ask the Lord to let His light shine into our lives. Is there anything in our life that He would not be happy with? In that process of building communion, we learn how to live in the character of Jesus.

Mark 12:30 And thou shalt love the Lord thy God with all thy heart, and with all thy soul, and with all thy mind, and with all thy strength: this *is* the first commandment.

It is in that time of communion that the fruit of the Spirit is established. It is always interesting to me that in a time of confrontation, people talk about gifts and power when they should talk about fruit and character. That is what confrontation is about. It is always about fruit and character, about the life of Jesus, not the power of Jesus. It is always about the life of Jesus, not the work of Jesus. When we are in confrontation, when we are under pressure, God is talking to us about fruit and character. In communion, the Lord works a new level of intimacy into our lives. Standing still under the hand of God, wanting His will to be fulfilled no matter what cost to ourselves, is one of the most intimate responses we can make to Him. Kneeling down to kiss the hand that hurts creates an intimacy that truly glorifies the Lord. When we choose to submit to the Lord in times of great adversity, it is because our hearts are crying out for intimacy and communion. Part of that closeness is a new level of prayer that arises out of a broken and contrite heart. We give God permission to touch anything in our lives, and we ask for His faithfulness to endure so that His will may be done. In communion, our behavior before God is moving us into godliness and righteousness. The character of Jesus becomes our prominent desire to be transformed into the image of Jesus.

Romans 12:1, 2 I beseech you therefore, brethren, by the mercies of God, that ye present your bodies a living sacrifice, holy, acceptable unto God, *which is* your reasonable service. And be not conformed to this world: but be ye transformed by the renewing of your mind, that ye may prove what *is* that good, and acceptable, and perfect, will of God.

Every day we receive His mercy, presenting ourselves to Him and asking for renewal of mind so that transformation can take place. As the pain and difficulty of confrontation abounds, so does the presence of God in transformation. Our minds are assailed by the adversity of our circumstances, but as we present ourselves humbly before His mercy, His thinking renews our mind. We live through one more day proving the will of God in transition. In communion, we learn to live in day-tight compartments before Him. As we present ourselves at the beginning of a new day, we gradually begin to experience the newness of life that God re-creates within.

Lamentations 3:21-26 This I recall to my mind, therefore have I hope. *It is of* the LORD'S mercies that we are not consumed, because his compassions fail not. *They are* new every morning: great *is* thy faithfulness. The LORD *is* my portion, saith my soul; therefore will I hope in him. The LORD *is* good unto them that wait for him, to the soul *that* seeketh him. *It is* good that *a man* should both hope and quietly wait for the salvation of the LORD.

As we grow in our personal communion with the Lord, then He becomes the central issue in the transition process. We are turned around from dwelling on the pain and loss to begin to understand and experience the gain of transformation. The presence of God begins to increase upon us. Worship begins to blossom and reach for new heights. Every church should write songs that signify the love of God in the time of trial. Every church should keep a journal that details the prophecies, vision statement, and mission of the church that makes up our corporate revelation and destiny. Added to that should be a record of God's dealings with the church in the transition process. Unity should become an issue in our hearts. We need to unite around our love for Jesus and ask the Holy Spirit to enable us to find new ways of loving and caring for one another. This will lead us into the second part of God's strategy.

The church is the dwelling place of God by the Spirit. He lives in our relationships, not in our meetings. It is the love or lack of it between God's people that attracts Him to us or denies Him access.

1 Peter 2:4-8 To whom coming, *as unto* a living stone, disallowed indeed of men, but chosen of God, *and* precious, Ye also, as lively stones, are built up a spiritual house, an holy priesthood, to offer up spiritual sacrifices, acceptable to God by Jesus Christ. Wherefore also it is contained in the scripture, Behold, I lay in Sion a chief corner stone, elect, precious: and he that believeth on him shall not be confounded. Unto you therefore which believe *he is* precious: but unto them which be disobedient, the stone which the builders disallowed, the same is made the head of the corner, And a stone of stumbling, and a rock of offence, *even to them* which stumble at the word, being disobedient: whereunto also they were appointed.

Ephesians 2:19-22 Now therefore ye are no more strangers and foreigners, but fellowcitizens with the saints, and of the household of God; And are built upon the foundation of the apostles and prophets, Jesus Christ himself being the chief corner *stone;* In whom all the building fitly framed together groweth unto an holy temple in the Lord: In whom ye also are builded together for an habitation of God through the Spirit.

The confrontation/transformation process has been designed by the Lord to increase the degree of fit between God's people.

Transition shapes and dresses our life so that we can successfully take our place alongside others. Transition squares us up and gets rid of all our rough edges, which prevent real unity from happening. The process destroys carnality and independence, and allows God's love to cement us together in a new bonding of love and friendship. It is so important to the Lord that we redefine our covenant together as people brought together to serve the purposes of God. Out of transition should come a new set of core values principles of loving relationship that we can fall back on in times of adversity, so that we never again fall prey to friction and divisiveness. Redefining our covenant walk together and re-establishing our core values are vital parts of coming out of transition into a new place before God as a church. In transition, the whole church (or as many as remain!) need to discuss together the issues of friendship and loving relationships.

We must, with great deliberation, think through what we want from our relationships and make covenant at a new level. Wherever our hearts are joined together with others, we must strengthen the ties that bind us together. Friends must talk openly of their love for one another and their desire for a stronger heart connection. Existing relationships must become more inclusive as we open our circle to involve fresh people. No one should be lonely. Those who are loners must be loved into submitting that side of their nature in order to evolve a relational lifestyle. We cannot change people's personalities. Some people are naturally more open and social. However, we all have to make relational adjustments in order to build a habitation for the Lord.

Covenant must be redefined around openness and honesty; non-negotiable love in times of adversity; believing the best of one another; making negative fellowship and criticism an offense against the house; looking out for one another; and considering others more important. Do everything to make God welcome! Redefine the servant-spirit heart of the church; talk about love and unity, sacrifice, mutual trust, and obedience to God on a corporate level. Come to the place of the early Church, who were of one mind, one heart, one accord, and all together. Make sure that the presence of God is your priority, not just His power. God is present when covenant is made and kept. He will test our covenant, so be prepared for that. We want to build a church that is so attractive to God that He cannot stay away. This kind of covenant can be forged only in the adversity of transition. We can design covenant at any time, but it can be made real only in adversity. It has to be tested. In adversity, real communion and covenant are forged in the house of the Lord. Testing makes it or breaks it. We must make sure that our relationships are strong enough to attract the presence of God as well as to endure the warfare that our corporate anointing will provoke. We all will be under attack in this new dimension. That is part of the adventure and the excitement of walking in a new place with God. We get to see a whole new level of His majesty and supremacy. We must learn how to stand together and fight for one another (as opposed to against each other!).

Luke 22:28 Ye are they which have continued with me in my temptations.

If our difficulties drive us apart, it is probably because we did not have much in the way of relationship and friendship. Real covenant is defined in times of danger, difficulty, and diversity. It is an unwritten law in relationships that all friendships will be tested. We have to know who our real friends are. Which friendship is only at a surface level? Which relationships are based around performance? If I am doing well and am successful, people flock around me, but if the wheels come off my wagon, do I have any real friends those who will ride the storm with me? We mostly make covenants or expressions of love and friendship in good times when all is well. Relational storms signify if our hearts are true. That is why God is dealing with the enemy within, dealing with our carnality, so that He can raise us to that level where we make covenant and live it out with each other. When the church is going through profound distress because God is sorting people out on the inside, the one thing that He will want to establish in that particular church is covenant. That is what our present distress is all about it is about us personally coming into greater communion with God and collectively coming in to covenant in the house of God. He will want to establish covenant in the time of distress. The enemy wants to split us apart, infiltrate, demoralize, subvert our relationships, divide, rule, and close down the church. God is looking for us all to come together, start standing together, and make a new covenant to the house of God. In distress, we must redefine covenant in our midst.

Don't wait until everything is going well; start looking at it right now. What is the process of covenant? Don't wait until things get better, because we could be hopelessly divided by then. The only way we move forward in this time of distress and attack of the enemy is by making covenant with each other. We choose to believe the best about each other, choose to stand together, choose to understand that this whole thing is the work of the cross and nothing more, and that we must allow God to deal with our hearts. Re-establishing the core values of God will become a matter of policy in our friendships. One of our major core values must be that we love each other no matter what is happening. Another is that in times of tension and difficulty, our love is non-negotiable. So if we are having differences in the leadership, our love is never on the negotiating table. We love each other no matter what, and we stay together. We are just having a difference of opinion, but we are committed 100 percent to each other. Loving each other is a core value and principle. We live together in relationships that are based on God's principles, not a worldly value system.

The world values success, wealth, position, status, good looks, and charisma. If those elements diminish in the world, friendship can fluctuate accordingly. God loves us according to His principled nature. He is unchanging in the way that He acts toward us. The loving-kindness of God is from everlasting to everlasting. It is fresh every morning. He forgives and He forgets. He is gracious and kind, slow to anger, swift to bless. His goodness and kindness enable us to apologize and be changed.

He practices the fruit of the Spirit in our lives! This is how God treats us in good times or in bad; when we are doing well or badly. How can we be any different from Him? In times of demoralization and stress, we must re-define our core values, for they are what we will hold onto while going through the storm. They are what will stop us from sinking into depravity and sin; they will prevent us from dividing and splitting off, breaking our covenant to the house of God. We are building relationships of mutual trust and honesty, of openness and obedience to God, of integrity, of love and unity, having a fervent spirit toward one another. We are living in sacrifice and being committed to each other. We are speaking those values out, living them out, and working them out in the violence of the situation that we are caught up in. In distress, as a church, we will discover who is really joined to us in heart and who is joined to the elation of what was happening in the meetings. When churches are expanded in the Spirit realm, they have an influx, an increase of people joining. Everyone wants to be where the anointing is present.

Every time expansion takes place it's followed by a period of contraction. Wait till the storm hits. Then see who remains faithful when God is pruning the work. It is a scriptural principle that after a time of heavy fruit, pruning must occur in order to increase our potential for future success. See who remains after pruning has taken place. These are your real disciples; anyone else was just hanging around. In times of blessing, all the spiritual nomads come out of the woodwork. In adversity, they will disappear. This is what we call "felt-led" poisoning. During times of blessing, people "feel led" to join us; during adversity, they "feel led" to go elsewhere. Such people are rootless and will never grow. They are clouds without rain. They have a form of godliness but no power. No root means no fruit. We simply cannot count on them. Of course, we are not denying the power of God to change such people. We do not start counting Christians until the storm is over! These people do not have any concept of sacrifice or faithfulness. They keep drinking out of someone else's well instead of digging their own. It is in times of difficulty when we learn what covenant is really all about. If all we are doing when the going gets tough is going somewhere else, we will never actually put down roots.

In transition, the leaders are going to be particularly vulnerable. They will be the main target of demonic attack from outside and fleshly involvement from inside the church. They need love, support, and prayer at this time. Instead, they will usually receive criticism, complaints, and accusations. They will come under attack in all kinds of subtle ways. Internally, some people may make a power play by seeking to undermine their leadership, authority, and gifting. This will usually come from within the leadership, from a particular ministry within the church, or from someone who feels that his gifting and ministry has not been promoted in the way he would like. Then there are the vultures from other churches leaders and ministries who feed off these types of situations. On the surface, they offer a shoulder for our people to cry on and sympathy with prayer and "prophetic counsel." It appears compassionate but lays the grasping power underneath. They will deny sheep stealing and simply say they are growing better grass. A thief is a thief. Most of this activity goes on in private and secret. I believe that we should be cautious about people joining us from other churches in the locality. We do not want to deny people the right to move on in the purpose of God; however, we must make sure that it is the purpose of God. Don't steal sheep. Birth some new ones out of the world. Transfer growth seldom works effectively. It can take years to work some things through with people unless we have a move of God upon them. Better to have fresh fish than someone else's people. I do realize that many people have been smoked by the ungodly fires of some leaders and ministries. I do not want to deny people a place of healing. However, they must be willing to eventually get healed, delivered, and move on in the purpose of God. In transition, there is a spirit of accusation that is dispatched to attack the leadership. Again, we must fall back on our core values in this type of situation. Most leaders will not have trod this path before, so mistakes will happen. Mistakes that arise out of ignorance and inadequacy are par for the course, entirely understandable, and easily forgiven.

Defend your leaders against the flesh and the demonic. Guard their back. We do not have to become "yes men" who live in perpetual agreement with leadership. We are allowed to have private disagreements as long as our love and commitment is not on the negotiating table if things do not work out how we want. Disagree by all means, but remain faithful to the core values of God. Pray for your leaders. If you are having it tough, they are probably having a harder time. One of the reasons churches split is because people stop praying for their leaders in the distress that they are experiencing. Leaders are vulnerable and human and need the protection and shield of our love and prayers.

Transition is a time when we should express our commitment to leaders and act it out. They need to know who they can count on in the battle that is raging. If we withdraw in seasons of trouble, we will never gain strength as a church to attack the enemy. They will not be right about everything. That clearly would be an unrealistic expectation. They are under immense pressure and will inevitably not see some things as they should. The grace of God can cover our mistakes as we go through transition. The valley is no place for making decisions. Let us try and leave, when possible, major decisions until we regain our balance. Transition is a character issue. Our leaders are taking hits in transition. They need a prayer shield. They need friends whom they can confide in, people who will knock out the dents in their armor. Leaders will need continual expressions of love before this thing is over. Their confidence may be fragile despite outward appearances. The violence of transition may last for months. The buildup of pressure will be huge, and leaders need somewhere to vent just as we all do. We don't have to get creepy on people and fawn all over them. Neither is this an opportunity to insinuate ourselves into any future power base. It is love for the sake of love. It is representing God's heart and capacity to bless, restore, and support. In times of continuous stress, our leaders need the Aarons and the Hurs to hold up their arms just as they did for Moses in the fight against a resourceful enemy.

Exodus 17:8-13 Then came Amalek, and fought with Israel in Rephidim. And Moses said unto Joshua, Choose us out men, and go out, fight with Amalek: to morrow I will stand on the top of the hill with the rod of God in mine hand. So Joshua did as Moses had said to him, and fought with Amalek: and Moses, Aaron, and Hur went up to the top of the hill. And it came to pass, when Moses held up his hand, that Israel prevailed: and when he let down his hand, Amalek prevailed. But Moses' hands *were* heavy; and they took a stone, and put *it* under him, and he sat thereon; and Aaron and Hur stayed up his hands, the one on the one side, and the other on the other side; and his hands were steady until the going down of the sun. And Joshua discomfited Amalek and his people with the edge of the sword.

Leaders need to know that God is protecting them and that people are believing the best and praying over their lives. Commitment to the leadership now in transition will enable us to develop the authority for future warfare as we take ground. In transition, we are defending the ground that we possess, but we also are developing the authority to increase our territory in the future. Something is forged in transition between leaders and the church. This is where God learns whether He can trust us and thrust us into the real battle for supremacy in the region. Stand together in faithfulness. Be faithful to the Lord, the vision, the house, and the leadership. The enemy will try and make you passive in your response to leaders. Be active in expression. Be visible in serving. Make it a joy for leaders to be over the church. Let your yes be a yes verbally! Expression deepens impression. Our ability to hold together during transition will strengthen our corporate character, causing a greater flow of sanctification and godliness. This is where we will begin to rule as we earn a place of trust with Almighty God.

In transition, we will need friends from outside who can provide objective support and care. We also need access to people who understand transition and process. In transition, we are re-digging the foundations of the church so that the Lord can erect a bigger building and release a greater dynamic of corporate power and identity. The only people who can really help us now are apostles and prophets. They are foundation ministries. It is inevitable in transition that our structures are going to change. New paradigms need to form as God delivers us from being a stereotype to a prototype church. Changes must come. We need prophetic insight and apostolic strategy combining together to re-develop the foundation and structure of the work. We will need external help to cultivate our core values and to re-define our friendships. We must suspend as much as we are able of our program in favor of meetings that will build, support, and sustain us through the process of change, for a season. The quality of relationships must improve or our corporate character will be diminished. Unity must be practiced. Trust must go to a deeper level. We need these external ministries to enable us to work through our differences. It is not just on the public platform that we need building ministries. It is in our discussions at leadership level. The new wineskin needs to be described by prophetic input from a building prophet. There are blessing prophets who are good in public meetings, speaking and prophesying over people. Only a building prophet can speak of the future in the violence of transition and inspire people to hold on together. A building prophet will make himself available to counsel, advise, and continuously inspire the church in this difficult period. Apostles and prophets together are the eye in the storm, bringing peace and order into chaos. They are a catalyst to provide breakthrough. By teaching, advice, prophecy, and impartation, they can furnish the building blocks to enable us to bridge the gap between where we are now and where we aspire to be.

Chapter Six
A New Church Arises In Manifestations

This is the finish stage of all transition stages. The manifestations are the fulfillment of all that God has promised. It is the most Glorious time of all transitions. The combined resources of apostle and prophet will bring us to the place in God where there is a release in the Spirit realm. In transition, our corporate identity will be released and a new life message will form. Manifestation is the fulfillment and the revealing of all that God declared to us in revelation at the onset of the process.

The Lord now trusts us enough to cause us to rise up and occupy a new place. Transformation has worked and our character has grown before God, giving Him confidence in our capacity to live at this new level. He gave us the original word, then plunged us into confrontation and transformation to enable our character to rise to a place where that word could be released. Now we fit the word that we have received, and a whole new realm of power and anointing will open up to us. We cannot merely pray down the presence of God; we must attract Him by the quality of our relationships.

We must become living stones fitted together into a house of God. The Lord is not looking for great meetings. He is looking for a house. If we build it, He will come! Through transformation we are made beautiful before the Lord. He becomes attracted to our holiness and love for one another. There is a blessing in unity that attracts the Holy Spirit. There is a curse in disunity that attracts the demonic. Worship begins to grow in our midst because we are falling more in love with Jesus. Our corporate identity and vision is re-established in our midst, and we inherit a season of divine acceleration. A quickening spirit is released that speeds up the new spiritual growth we need, to occupy this new place. Time that we thought would be lost and wasted in transition is now mysteriously made up as God commits Himself to manifestation in our midst. People begin to grow and accelerate in the Spirit. Faith begins to be magnified in people's hearts as they hear the Lord in a fresh way. We come to that place in our occupation where souls begin to fall into the Kingdom. There is an anointing upon individuals to witness; there is an anointing on the church to reap the harvest that God is actually giving us. We will find that all the people around us who God has been preparing, unbeknownst to us, suddenly start coming to the church and finding the Lord.

God starts digging us wells on housing developments where we never had a presence. He gives us property in places where we never actually thought of moving to. All sorts of things begin to happen around us. God begins to give us our inheritance and the land along with it.

He enlarges our boundaries in the natural as well as in the spiritual. Suddenly, our territory increases because, in confrontation, God transformed us and now is trusting us, actually marking out our inheritance and territory. God is the original territorial spirit. The enemy is just a copy. God is territorial.

Deuteronomy 11:24 Every place whereon the soles of your feet shall tread shall be yours: from the wilderness and Lebanon, from the river, the river Euphrates, even unto the uttermost sea shall your coast be.

That is a territorial spirit at work. The devil has never done anything original. All he does is copy God. God is a territorial spirit, so the devil wants to be one as well. God will give us our inheritance, and we will find our territory will begin to increase. Everything we come into now will come to us through the warfare of transition. Don't be frightened of this whole process, which God loves; He knows the place it will lead us to. He will walk us through it hand in hand. We will discover God in ways that we never thought we would ever know Him during time. I have worked with churches in transition for a number of years, and I love the whole process. I find it remarkable. It is fascinating to help churches begin to see God in a way they never understood Him before. They begin to experience God and come to a place where they realize that nothing can hurt them. Nothing can touch them. This is where their anointing in warfare and battle really gets birthed in their hearts. We begin learning about what it is to rely on the presence of God and on the person of God. When we make space for the King of kings, His presence with us gives incredible heart and faith to enable us to press through transition. When He comes, He comes in power and in faith. Even the whispers of God will cause great faith to rise. When the presence of God comes, everything comes with Him.

We are going to become a church that moves in the manifest presence of God. But first, we have to be conformed to His image and that happens only through confrontation. The prophecy and vision we received in revelation now begin to unfold. Divine appointments begin to happen. God is in the house and in control!

In the violence of confrontation, there will be some people who will leave us. Some will be fair-weather friends and perhaps no great loss. Others may be leaders and ministries key people in the work in spiritual, financial, and relational terms. We may lose friends and people whom we have come to depend on. All our resources will come under attack. Whatever the prophetic promises about resources and anointing that God will release to us, we will suffer a contraction before we experience expansion. It is a grievous experience when we know that people who should have known better, leave us and go elsewhere people who have a level of maturity and wisdom but cannot see the point of what is happening. Some leave because of personal ambition. Others leave for a quieter life and greener pastures. People whom we thought were anchor points are now no longer there, and we feel adrift in a sea of turmoil. Surprising things happen in transition. Anchor people leave, and those who were drifting suddenly put down roots and are a stabilizing influence. Adversity changes people for the better as well as the worst. The devil steals people away from the work, but not everyone who leaves is deceived. Some leave legitimately in God. Many, though, are taken from us, and we cannot endorse their departure. In manifestation, the Lord makes the enemy pay for his handiwork.

Exodus 22:1 If a man shall steal an ox, or a sheep, and kill it, or sell it; he shall restore five oxen for an ox, and four sheep for a sheep.

An ox is a working animal and therefore represents a leader or a key gift in the church. A sheep represents a church member. I believe we have permission at this time to ask for retribution and repayment. Look back over the period of transition to people who have been lost to us. For every gifted person and leader, we want five caliber replacements. For every church member lost, we want four new people. This is important! To really pay the enemy back, we must ask the Lord for replacements at the new level we are occupying. We do not want replacement people at the old pre-transition level. We want people who can be a resource now at this new level. We are asking for an increase of people with the capacity to inherit and minister in the new land of occupation. We need to make the enemy regret all that he did against us! We must come together before the Lord in the manner of the widow.

Luke 18:1-8 And he spake a parable unto them *to this end, that men ought always to pray, and not to faint; Saying, There was in a city a judge, which feared not God, neither regarded man: And there was a widow in that city; and she came unto him, saying, Avenge me of mine adversary. And he would not for a while: but afterward he said within himself, Though I fear not God, nor regard man; Yet because this widow troubleth me, I will avenge her, lest by her continual coming she weary me. And the Lord said, Hear what the unjust judge saith. And shall not God avenge his own elect, which cry day and night unto him, though he bear long with them? I tell you that he will avenge them speedily. Nevertheless when the Son of man cometh, shall he find faith on the earth?*

He refused to give it many times. The widow finally received justice from him because of her persistence. Note that her cry was

"Avenge me of my adversary!" God is the exact opposite of this unrighteous judge. He is not unwilling to hear us. However, we need to come before Him with persistence to request that He judges the enemy on our behalf.

We must ask for a restoration of new people at the new level. We must ask for retribution according to,

Luke 22:1 Now the feast of unleavened bread drew nigh, which is called the Passover.

We want resource church people who will fit us now and add immediate weight to current spiritual developments. Ask and keep on asking. Some of these people will join us from elsewhere. Others will suddenly accelerate growth from within. Do not stop praying until these people are present. Enjoy this time in particular.

Isaiah 61:2 To proclaim the acceptable year of the LORD, and the day of vengeance of our God; to comfort all that mourn;

Above all, enjoy this new place in the Spirit. Learn to bask in the warmth of God's favor and blessing. This is a new day! The New Church is Arising as the Prototype Church that will be Glorious.

Chapter Seven
The Royal Process

Most of the Church today has not found their ability and authority of Heaven. The Kingly Royal Process is the anointing power and authority of all of Heaven at your word. We must allow God to take us through the process of royalty. This will accelerate you to the place you're supposed to be in God.

I have a burning awareness that it's time for us to put away childish things so that we come to maturity and advance as kings and priests bearing the authority that the Lord intends for us to possess.

1 Corinthians 13:11 When I was a child, I spake as a child, I understood as a child, I thought as a child: but when I became a man, I put away childish things.

God is roaring against His enemies, pushing them back, so that Christians will have greater freedom to rise up into their destiny as kings and priests. God's plan is that we march as a mighty army in these last days.

I want to speak about three things that happen-prophetic promises-when the Lion of the tribe of Judah roars. I believe there's going to come an impartation of an anointing for a release of the roar of the Lion of the tribe of Judah in our spirit today. When the Lion of the tribe of Judah roars it actually sets the captives free. In the spirit there is a release for those who sit in darkness to come forth into freedom in Christ.

The prophet Hosea prophesied that Ephraim symbolizing our prodigal sons and daughters would walk after the Lord and follow His ways after the lion roars.

Hosea 11:8-11 How shall I give thee up, Ephraim? *how* shall I deliver thee, Israel? how shall I make thee as Admah? *how* shall I set thee as Zeboim? mine heart is turned within me, my repentings are kindled together. I will not execute the fierceness of mine anger, I will not return to destroy Ephraim: for I *am* God, and not man; the Holy One in the midst of thee: and I will not enter into the city. They shall walk after the LORD: he shall roar like a lion: when he shall roar, then the children shall tremble from the west. They shall tremble as a bird out of Egypt, and as a dove out of the land of Assyria: and I will place them in their houses, saith the LORD.

When there is a release of the roar in Zion, not only is there a release of the captive sons and daughters, but there is actually a planting of destiny. They come and they dwell in the house of the Lord and there is a rooting that takes place when the lion roars. Wouldn't you like the Lion to roar over your family and just shake the darkness loose? I believe this roar is being released even today on behalf of the prodigals. So I want you to receive that as a prophetic promise. When the Lion of the tribe of Judah roars there is a pronunciation of judgment on our enemies.

The prophet Joel prophesied about a war when many nations would come to the valley of Jehoshaphat where God will sit to judge all the surrounding nations.

Joel 3:12 Let the heathen be wakened, and come up to the valley of Jehoshaphat: for there will I sit to judge all the heathen round about.

Then he speaks about the Lord roaring from Zion against Israel's enemies, but the Lord will be a shelter for His people:

Joel 3:16 The LORD also shall roar out of Zion, and utter his voice from Jerusalem; and the heavens and the earth shall shake: but the LORD *will be* the hope of his people, and the strength of the children of Israel.

Yes, there is a judgment that comes against our enemies when the Lion roars from Zion, but we need to keep in mind that we'll find shelter in the time of judgment only when we're walking in humility with complete devotion to the Lord.

When the Lion of the tribe of Judah roars there is a call and stirring of violence and war. The prophet Isaiah prophesied concerning this when he says that the Lord will come down and fight for Mt. Zion and for its hill.

Isaiah 31:4 For thus hath the LORD spoken unto me, Like as the lion and the young lion roaring on his prey, when a multitude of shepherds is called forth against him, *he* will not be afraid of their voice, nor abase himself for the noise of them: so shall the LORD of hosts come down to fight for mount Zion, and for the hill thereof.

This passage of Scripture speaks of aggression and stirs within us a response to the call for the mighty warriors to rise up.

In the natural, when the lion roars, the prey is frozen with fear so the lioness can go in and take the prey. Let's get a revelation about this because it's a strategy in warfare. The roar of the lion paralyzes and causes fear and dread in the enemy's camp so that we, the lioness, can take our prey. God is going to release in our spirit an increase in the level of authority in aggressive spiritual warfare that will immobilize the enemy's plans.

The prophet Isaiah prophesied about a never-ending increase!

Isaiah 9:7 Of the increase of *his* government and peace *there shall be* no end, upon the throne of David, and upon his kingdom, to order it, and to establish it with judgment and with justice from henceforth even for ever. The zeal of the LORD of hosts will perform this.

Isaiah 9:6 For unto us a child is born, unto us a son is given: and the government shall be upon his shoulder: and his name shall be called Wonderful, Counsellor, The mighty God, The everlasting Father, The Prince of Peace.

God invites us to co-labor with Him in the administration of His government in the earth and He gives us a kingly, priestly anointing to carry this through. The government of God is coming and it's already happening, all at the same time! Our faith at this point causes action.

James 2:17 Even so faith, if it hath not works, is dead, being alone.

In fact, there is a principle here. Our destinies are established in the Heavenlies already, but we must contend for our destinies and cooperate with God to bring them into existence in our everyday lives.

The prophet Isaiah connects the never-ending increase of God's government with the throne of David, so let's take a look at King David's life. God chose David to be the king of Israel when he was just a young man.

1Samuel 16:1-13 And the LORD said unto Samuel, How long wilt thou mourn for Saul, seeing I have rejected him from reigning over Israel? fill thine horn with oil, and go, I will send thee to Jesse the Bethlehemite: for I have provided me a king among his sons. And Samuel said, How can I go? if Saul hear *it*, he will kill me. And the LORD said, Take an heifer with thee, and say, I am come to sacrifice to the LORD. And call Jesse to the sacrifice, and I will shew thee what thou shalt do: and thou shalt anoint unto me *him* whom I name unto thee. And Samuel did that which the LORD spake, and came to Bethlehem. And the elders of the town trembled at his coming, and said, Comest thou peaceably? And he said, Peaceably: I am come to sacrifice unto the LORD: sanctify yourselves, and come with me to the sacrifice. And he sanctified Jesse and his sons, and called them to the sacrifice. And it came to pass, when they were come, that he looked on Eliab, and said, Surely the LORD'S anointed *is* before him. But the LORD said unto Samuel, Look not on his countenance, or on the height of his stature; because I have refused him: for *the LORD seeth* not as man seeth; for man looketh on the outward appearance, but the LORD looketh on the heart. Then Jesse called Abinadab, and made him pass before Samuel. And he said, Neither hath the LORD chosen this. Then Jesse made Shammah to pass by. And he said, Neither hath the LORD chosen this. Again, Jesse made seven of his sons to pass before Samuel. And Samuel said unto Jesse, The LORD hath not chosen these. And Samuel said unto Jesse, Are here all *thy* children? And he said, There remaineth yet the youngest, and, behold, he keepeth the sheep. And Samuel said unto Jesse, Send and fetch him: for we will not sit down till he come hither. And he sent, and brought him in. Now he *was* ruddy, *and* withal of a beautiful countenance, and goodly to look to. And the LORD said, Arise, anoint him: for this *is* he. Then Samuel took the horn of oil, and anointed him in the midst of his brethren: and the Spirit of the LORD came upon David from that day forward. So Samuel rose up, and went to Ramah.

The Lord told Samuel the prophet to go to the house of Jesse because He had selected one of Jesse's sons to be King over Israel. And so Samuel did as he was told. But the seven sons who came before him, even though each one looked like a possible contender; they didn't have the goods and were eliminated by the Lord. So Samuel asked Jesse if he had any more children. He must have been relieved to learn there was one son left, the youngest, who wasn't at home. And so the remaining son, David, was summoned from tending the sheep. Immediately when Samuel laid his eyes on David the Lord said, Arise, anoint him; for this is the one. The prophet poured the oil on David and he was anointed as King, long before he experienced the full manifestation of living as a king. David was chosen called by God. In the midst of all his brothers, there was favor. The Bible also says, The Spirit of the Lord came upon him from that day forward. He was the King of Israel because the ministry of God came to him. However, after being anointed King, David finds himself thrust into several life and death experiences. And he encounters great favor with King Saul for a season, but this favor changes into deadly disfavor to the point that

David becomes an outlaw. He's forced to run like a dog into the wilderness, hiding in the caves. While he's hiding out in the caves 400 disgruntled guys come to his side.

1 Samuel 22:2 And every one *that was* in distress, and every one that *was* in debt, and every one *that was* discontented, gathered themselves unto him; and he became a captain over them: and there were with him about four hundred men.

They came to David when he was having a difficult time. You know, when hard times come, we find out who are friends are. David's new friends weren't attracted to his posh home and financial prosperity! At this point in David's life, his great wealth was his reputation-a bold warrior and a man of great character. He single handedly slew Goliath and he didn't retaliate when Saul tried to kill him. These disgruntled guys saw something emerging in David that marked him as a great leader and this drew them to his side. Yes, they were angry outcasts who were somewhat bitter, but they had discernment. They knew a good leader when they saw one. How many of us have heard great things about our destiny, too, just like King David? How long Lord? When Lord?

Some of us have been waiting for many years for the fulfillment of what we know the Lord has purposed for our lives. And we're having an experience like David had after he was anointed as king. It appears that he received everything from God to fulfill the call on his life, but for years he didn't have the full manifestation of ruling the kingdom yet. David was in training and adversity was having its perfect work; he wasn't rebelling against it. David was proving to be a true king, one trained in the wilderness. David's wilderness experience was pretty rough. He was probably thinking: I don't look like a king and I don't feel like a king.

What kind of kingdom is this? But he begins to take the rejects and trains their hands for war in the wilderness. He's an outcast; like a dog on the run. Saul wants to kill him. He's thinking: How am I ever going to get from point A to point B? How am I ever going to be King? Life goes on like that for a few more years! He experiences a lot of warfare in the wilderness.

Psalms 63:1 **A Psalm of David, when he was in the wilderness of Judah.** O God, thou *art* my God; early will I seek thee: my soul thirsteth for thee, my flesh longeth for thee in a dry and thirsty land, where no water is;

Seeking God early, being thirsty for His presence when it's dry, not giving up when all outward signs seem to indicate defeat; this describes wilderness warfare. There isn't a hint of revival; no special meetings and no sense of the presence of God. Do you know what water is in the Bible? Water is the Holy Ghost. I will open rivers in desolate heights, and fountains in the midst of the valleys; I will make the wilderness a pool of water, and the dry land springs of water.

Isaiah 41:18 I will open rivers in high places, and fountains in the midst of the valleys: I will make the wilderness a pool of water, and the dry land springs of water.

Devils don't like the water and they leave us alone when we get wet in the Holy Ghost! They like the dry places.

Mark 5:12 And all the devils besought him, saying, Send us into the swine, that we may enter into them.

Jesus allowed this because He knew that when the hoard entered the pigs, they would rush down the hill into the sea, into the water, the very place demons hate. One day they will be in the LAKE of fire! Not only is Jesus an expert when it comes to dealing with demons, He provides for us in the wilderness when it's dry and there's no water. ...I will even make a road in the wilderness and rivers in the desert.

Isaiah 43:19 Behold, I will do a new thing; now it shall spring forth; shall ye not know it? I will even make a way in the wilderness, *and* rivers in the desert.

Did you know that sometimes a river isn't just flowing with water; it's flowing with grace? If we'll receive grace, God will pour it on us like a river of blessing: Thus says the Lord, The people who survived the sword found grace in the wilderness-Israel, when it went to find its rest.

Jeremiah 31:12 Therefore they shall come and sing in the height of Zion, and shall flow together to the goodness of the LORD, for wheat, and for wine, and for oil, and for the young of the flock and of the herd: and their soul shall be as a watered garden; and they shall not sorrow any more at all.

Sometimes when we're in the wilderness it's tempting to rebel and throw in the towel. Even when God comes and makes us an offer of grace, we just don't like it at all! We don't want grace in the wilderness. We want OUT of there, like YESTERDAY! David's lifestyle proves that he received a big dose of grace from the Holy Spirit. His attitude can be ours as we take a look at what his thought-life was probably like: I've got these 400 outcasts around me. God, I'm so hungry for You! God, I'm so hungry for Your glory!

I'm so hungry for Your power! Even in a dry and thirsty land where there's no water. I'm going to dig diligently! I am not going to let up or shut up! I'm not going to give up in this wilderness!

Chapter Eight
Kingly Character

David is one that I have learned so much of. He was an underdog that God picked because of his heart and character. David persevered in the wilderness. This proved his character and pictures what Paul the apostle taught when he said:

Romans 5:3, 4 And not only *so*, but we glory in tribulations also: knowing that tribulation worketh patience; And patience, experience; and experience, hope:

When God saw David's character maturing steadily, producing great fruit, He decided to do some pruning, and every branch that bears fruit, He prunes it so that it may bear more fruit.

John 15:2 Every branch in me that beareth not fruit he taketh away: and every *branch* that beareth fruit, he purgeth it, that it may bring forth more fruit.

And so after a long season of pruning fighting, training his men and running from Saul-David is led by the Lord to Hebron where he is anointed King over the house of Judah and then later he's anointed King over Israel. It's in Hebron where David begins to experience more of the manifestation of the kingly anointing. It's like God is saying: I trust you with more in this next season. Now you're going to go from the wilderness with trained men, rather than discontented bums and outcasts. You trained their hands for war! You were faithful. I am going to bring an increase of authority upon your life and it's going to intensify in Hebron.

Do you know what Hebron is? Hebron means the city of four and seat of association. Even to this day, Hebron is a city struggling with a lot of spiritual warfare. Historically, when the 12 spies went into Canaan they eventually came into the Negev region to Hebron where the descendants of Anak lived:

Numbers 13:22 And they ascended by the south, and came unto Hebron; where Ahiman, Sheshai, and Talmai, the children of Anak, *were*. (Now Hebron was built seven years before Zoan in Egypt.)

Anak means to choke, strangle and struggle with death. Ahiman means to block or hinder. Sheshai means to whiten or white wash.

These sons were giants in the land. After the children of Israel wandered in the wilderness for 40 years, when they finally came into their inheritance under Joshua's leadership, Caleb asked for Hebron as his inheritance. Caleb said that with the Lord's help he would drive out the giants, the sons of Anak. And he did just that! Caleb was 85 years old then and as strong as an ox!

Joshua 15:14 And Caleb drove thence the three sons of Anak, Sheshai, and Ahiman, and Talmai, the children of Anak.

Throughout the Scriptures we see the children of Israel having to deal with demonic powers similar to the ones in Anakim's three sons. Just like King David had to persevere through the caves and wilderness and overcome different giants, so do we. God will use all the difficulties He allows in our lives as resistance to build our spiritual muscles. When the enemy tries to choke us to death and hinder us from moving ahead; when he tries to white wash everything so we just settle for less; we need to rise up and fight back with God's strategy! We need to contend for our destinies.

When the enemy tries to white wash something, it's like our vision isn't clear and we don't see things on the outside as they really are.

Matthew 23:27 Woe unto you, scribes and Pharisees, hypocrites! for ye are like unto whited sepulchres, which indeed appear beautiful outward, but are within full of dead *men's* bones, and of all uncleanness.

To white wash means: settle for it; it looks good; take your lot in life, or grin and bear it! We got this complacent, settle for, aw it's out there and it doesn't affect me so that's good enough, mentality. There's got to be a manifestation of aggression. There has to be a rising up. There's got to be this spiritual violence. The violent take it by force.

Matthew 11:12 And from the days of John the Baptist until now the kingdom of heaven suffereth violence, and the violent take it by force.

We need to change our mindset: I'm going to press in and I'm going to set the standard! I'm going to get a breakthrough! When it's hard and dry I'm going to worship and cry out to God all the more. When the blessing isn't manifesting and the oil isn't here, You are still worthy Lord! I will keep contending for my destiny! My whole attitude can be summed up like this: I'm going to serve God! I'm going to be a radical, extravagant lover of God! David was in the wilderness; all true kings need to go there. When God promoted David by sending him to Hebron, he would experience even more of the pruning process so that he could bear much fruit as the king of Israel. It was like the Lord said to David; I am going to increase you. You passed the test! Go to Hebron! There, in that place, David would rise even higher as a trusted leader, contending for his kingly anointing.

We saw that when David emerged as an outstanding leader, God promoted him and changed his home base to Hebron where he was anointed King of Judah. In this new location he was surrounded by even more intense spiritual warfare because Anak's descendants lived there. These wicked descendants created a nesting place for darkness. New levels, new devils! How would you like the kind of promotion that by its very nature, just seems to invite great difficulties? Most of us would never sign up for hard times, but God knows that adversity builds both our character and our spiritual muscles.

Psalms 119:75 I know, O LORD, that thy judgments *are* right, and *that* thou in faithfulness hast afflicted me.

King David's promotion worked to his advantage because he gained great strength and wisdom in Hebron, overcoming many enemies both in the natural and spiritual realms. God didn't want David just to camp in Hebron for a few days. Rather, it was a necessary place to live so that he could grow in maturity for the next leg of his journey. God designed David's pilgrimage to include many difficulties, on purpose. He knew that adversity would prepare him to reign in the kingly anointing from Zion, the city of Jerusalem.

Psalms 84:5-7 Blessed *is* the man whose strength *is* in thee; in whose heart *are* the ways *of them. Who* passing through the valley of Baca make it a well; the rain also filleth the pools. They go from strength to strength, *every one of them* in Zion appeareth before God.

His heart attitude always wanted to please God and that was the focus that motivated him.

King David eventually left Hebron and was anointed King over Israel, reigning from Jerusalem.

2 Samuel 5:3-7 So all the elders of Israel came to the king to Hebron; and king David made a league with them in Hebron before the LORD: and they anointed David king over Israel. David *was* thirty years old when he began to reign, *and* he reigned forty years. In Hebron he reigned over Judah seven years and six months: and in Jerusalem he reigned thirty and three years over all Israel and Judah. And the king and his men went to Jerusalem unto the Jebusites, the inhabitants of the land: which spake unto David, saying, Except thou take away the blind and the lame, thou shalt not come in hither: thinking, David cannot come in hither. Nevertheless David took the strong hold of Zion: the same *is* the city of David.

He walked in the kingly anointing. So David went on and became great, and the Lord God of hosts was with him.

2 Samuel 5:10 And David went on, and grew great, and the LORD God of hosts *was* with him.

But before David ever became King, although he wasn't part of the Levitical priesthood like Aaron (Moses' brother) and Zadok the son of Ahitub, he possessed the heart of a priest.

You know, the function of a priest is very much like that of a pastor, and pastors are also called shepherds. So it's not surprising that David's heart (as a priest) would go hand in hand with his role as a shepherd. He was a true protector over his family's flock of sheep; an excellent shepherd. He didn't flinch when it came to making sure each little sheep was safe. When a prowling lion or bear approached his flock, he laid down his life and fought the intruders.

1 Samuel 17:36 Thy servant slew both the lion and the bear: and this uncircumcised Philistine shall be as one of them, seeing he hath defied the armies of the living God.

God saw him from heaven above like a proud Father watching His child. He knew that because David laid down his life for the sheep when no one was looking, he'd do it when they were looking. David had a passionate heart; he was a lover of God, one who desired deep intimacy with Him. When no one was around, David would take his stringed instrument and compose psalms and hymns. He probably danced wildly in the pastures, too! You see, God is watching what we do in secret. I meet these guys and they have this face that they put on when they're in a ministry position. They think: I'm going to church; it's Sunday. I got a position and a job to do. The pastor gave me 10 minutes this morning to speak. And all week they don't pray. It's like the preacher who preaches because it's his job. He's not concerned before the meeting to take time to soak and seek the Lord to be sure that he has something that God wants him to say. I'll just pull out something that I already have. But David was like a priest because he had the heart of a priest and this was what God was looking for.

When we have the heart of a faithful priest, then we have the right foundation so that God can increase our level of authority and bring us into a kingly anointing. And there is a great responsibility that comes with the priestly anointing. The Bible records that the Lord spoke to Eli (the priest) concerning his two sons because they didn't have the faithful hearts required of a priest. In fact they acted wickedly. They despised the things of God to the point that God was forced to pronounce His judgment against them.

1 Samuel 2:31, 32 Behold, the days come, that I will cut off thine arm, and the arm of thy father's house, that there shall not be an old man in thine house. And thou shalt see an enemy *in my* habitation, in all *the wealth* which *God* shall give Israel: and there shall not be an old man in thine house for ever.

But God did show compassion to Eli when He said that He would raise up a faithful priest and anyone who was left in Eli's household would be permitted to approach him.

1 Samuel 2:35, 36 And I will raise me up a faithful priest, *that* shall do according to *that* which *is* in mine heart and in my mind: and I will build him a sure house; and he shall walk before mine anointed for ever. And it shall come to pass, *that* every one that is left in thine house shall come *and* crouch to him for a piece of silver and a morsel of bread, and shall say, Put me, I pray thee, into one of the priests' offices, that I may eat a piece of bread.

A faithful priest in God's eyes is a servant who will do what is in His heart and mind.

Now I want to ask a question. How can we do what's in God's heart and mind, only doing those things that we see the Father doing, if we don't take the time to see what the Father's doing?

John 5:19 Then answered Jesus and said unto them, Verily, verily, I say unto you, The Son can do nothing of himself, but what he seeth the Father do: for what things soever he doeth, these also doeth the Son likewise.

We have to seek the heart and mind of God. A faithful priest isn't concerned about his own agendas and how he looks in public; it's about who he is in his heart. Eli functioned as a priest during the days when the word of the Lord was rare and visions were infrequent.

1 Samuel 3:1 And the child Samuel ministered unto the LORD before Eli. And the word of the LORD was precious in those days; *there was* no open vision.

His eyes were so dim that he couldn't see. This really is a picture of his spiritual condition. It's in this context that the boy Samuel (who was in Eli's care) ministers to the Lord and the word of the Lord begins to come to him. When God began to call Samuel's name, he thought it was Eli calling. Three times Samuel came to Eli, and it took Eli that long in his prophetic sensitivity to think, maybe this is God.

1 Samuel 3:4-8 That the LORD called Samuel: and he answered, Here *am* I. And he ran unto Eli, and said, Here *am* I; for thou calledst me. And he said, I called not; lie down again. And he went and lay down. And the LORD called yet again, Samuel. And Samuel arose and went to Eli, and said, Here *am* I; for thou didst call me. And he answered, I called not, my son; lie down again. Now Samuel did not yet know the LORD, neither was the word of the LORD yet revealed unto him. And the LORD called Samuel again the third time. And he arose and went to Eli, and said, Here *am* I; for thou didst call me. And Eli perceived that the LORD had called the child.

After all the years of walking in God's presence, what happened to Eli? I believe that He neglected to lie down where God's presence was and this resulted in Eli's household having no regard for God's holiness. The true priestly anointing always reflects the holiness of God and it's nourished in God's presence.

Chapter Nine
The New Church

Today the Church as a whole is experiencing a barrenness of fruit. What causes barrenness in Church life? When we talk about putting down roots or laying foundations, we often think of staying put in one place.

In the Bible the supernatural was commonplace. Men and women both spoke with sharpness and clarity in their representation of God. Words were backed up with power and anointing that saved lives and brought deliverance from occult powers, famines, disasters, and human oppression. This essence of pure relationship and raw power between God and His people has been the dominating theme of the Scriptures. Only the form and style have changed throughout the generations from a handmade stone altar roughly put together with materials on hand by individual men such as Abraham, Jacob, and the prophets, to the designer places of worship expressed in the tabernacle and temple. At times these places of worship were inspired by a revelation of God's grace, mercy, and calling, such as when Jacob-in-transition to-Israel finally came to understand the desire that God had for relationship with him. In other times and places, altars were built upon the sites of intense spiritual warfare and upon battlefields as sacrifices were offered to God on the burning embers of false gods and idol worship. Mount Carmel and Gideon's hometown became places of cleansing and purification as the enemy was driven out and the name of the Lord revealed.

From the Old Covenant to the New was established in the person of Jesus, who became the temple of God wandering amongst a guilty and sin-ridden people. Destroy this temple and God will raise it up in three days, He said, referring to Himself. Something had happened in the hearts of the people between times.

John 2:19 Jesus answered and said unto them, Destroy this temple, and in three days I will raise it up.

A creeping institution had given way to form without power, to style without substance, and to a performance mentality that elevated men, not God, in the presence of the people. People did things to be seen of others; rules of behavior governed the lives of many. Leaders had become blind guides, searching the Scriptures without prophetic insight. Those who most desired the coming of the Messiah missed Him because their interpretation of Scripture was not mingled with worship, the manifest presence of God, and prophetic wisdom. God walked among them, but they had not been trained to recognize His presence. All their teaching and distilled wisdom down through the years had left them without the faculty for discerning the glory of God. Even when they saw signs and wonders and Jesus graciously asked them to believe in those signs as part of their journey to a wider, deeper revelation of God's presence, they could not bring themselves to part from their institutional mind-sets. So the early Church grew up next to a narrow-minded institution that continued thinking that it alone held the glorious tradition of the truth of God. The old persecuted the new, which in turn eventually came against the newer works, which in time grew to be the oppressors of new moves of God till the present day.

The history of the Church are littered with stories of new moves of God erupting in the earth through orthodox persecution and then settling back into conventional, narrow-minded religiosity. Only the presence of God can prevent institutional Christianity from reducing truth to a set of rules and worship or to a meaningless time of singing without awe. Only God's presence can enable believers to confront the enemy and the evils of mankind with a powerful expression of truth combined with supernatural power. Only God's presence is the glue that holds us all together through tensions, conflicts, and the violence of being on the front line of the battle against a depraved and intimidating foe. We have lost the glory, the majesty, and the mystery of all that God is within Himself. The temple gave way to the synagogue and the mystery began to fade. Word stopped leading us to worship, and in time the dynamic revelation of God became a route to live by as we waited for God to come in final deliverance. Today's worship precedes the Word and in many places has become the platform for the teaching and the ministry of people. Our churches have lost the art of ministering to the Lord in worship and discerning the voice of the Lord in our midst.

Acts 13:1, 2 Now there were in the church that was at Antioch certain prophets and teachers; as Barnabas, and Simeon that was called Niger, and Lucius of Cyrene, and Manaen, which had been brought up with Herod the tetrarch, and Saul. As they ministered to the Lord, and fasted, the Holy Ghost said, Separate me Barnabas and Saul for the work whereunto I have called them.

People went to the temple to participate in the mystery and the majesty of God. They went for three main reasons: to worship, to make an offering, and to pray. In the synagogue they went to hear the word of God, to get their needs met, and to have fellowship. In the temple, the instruction and communication of God's word always led them into an experience with God. In the synagogue, it often led them into debate and discussion about God. Meetings became man-centered instead of revolving around the presence of God. Even today in many of the newer churches, if the meeting has a lot of content and activity, it is often the worship that gets squeezed. People go to church for good teaching or fellowship.

Our society has created intense loneliness, and people are hungry for companionship. Accordingly, it is easy to justify making our meetings into a designer-style atmosphere to attract people. I am not against this in principle. I think all our meetings should be aimed specifically at God's desire to do particular things and achieve specific objectives. I am against stereotypes that do not bring us into the creative presence of God. We must regain the capacity to live in the manifest presence of God. The teaching of the Word must lead people into an encounter of God Himself, not just into an experience of the church. God has always set people within the framework of tabernacle, temple, and church who would act as catalysts to cause breakthrough into the manifest presence of the Lord. When people look at us, they should see Jesus. They should observe His love in the way that we live together.

The entrance of God's Word should produce hope, faith, life, and health to every part of our being. The presence of God is life to us. When we lose His presence or, even worse, if we have never grown up with the reality of His glory, it is inevitable that we would use the Word to relegate the supernatural to a future time of glory in Heaven rather than glory now. God sits outside of time. He has not ever been full of glory. He is altogether glorious. Everything He touches carries the fragrance and the passion of His manifest presence. He is wonderful, awe-inspiring, and magnificent. Our meetings must reflect the glory of His unchanging nature.

I love to meditate on the nature and character of the Lord. For me, He has come to be the kindest person I have ever known. He is kindhearted, gracious, loving, good-natured, and benevolent. He is generous, cordial, approachable, and thoughtful. He is slow to anger and swift to bless. He sees the good, acknowledging the treasure and the worth in people. He inspires confidence, renews our self-worth, and puts a smile on our hearts. He is captivating, beautiful, and completely lovely. He is strong, powerful, a force to be reckoned with, a conqueror and overcomer. He is a paradox a fierce and mighty warrior dressed as a lamb; the king of glory and a bruised reed; a son, a servant, a prophet, a priest, and a king. The fear of Him is the beginning of wisdom, yet His laughter makes us move about with pleasure. He continually brings us to points of vulnerability and weakness so that His sheer joy in Himself can be our source of strength. Our meetings very often do not reflect His nature, but ours. They focus on our needs instead of celebrating who He is in our midst. How many of our people take time out during the day to spend just a few minutes in silent worship and awe of God? Whatever God is, He is infinitely. It is impossible for God not to be everlasting, endless, and eternal. He is the greatest endless and eternal expression of goodness, kindness, and grace.

He is everlastingly kind and merciful, eternally loving. He loves infinitely and without boundaries. There is no end to the kindness of God. He is also totally perfect. He never does anything partway. He completes everything He starts.

Philippians 1:6 Being confident of this very thing, that he which hath begun a good work in you will perform *it* until the day of Jesus Christ:

He does everything perfectly. He is infinitely good and perfectly good. He has perfect love and grace. His love is complete, wholesome, and endlessly perfect! He is always loving because He is infinite and perfect. He is immutable. He never changes. What God was, God is and God will be. There is no shadow of turning within Him. He is unchanging. What a relief! We all have experienced the fluctuating fortunes of human relationships and been both blessed and burned. I love the ongoing continuity of God's affection for me. He put me in the one place where I could relate to Him in all of my changeableness. He put me into Christ so that His unchanging, infinite, and perfect love could become a constant to me as I grew up in Him. He is never indifferent. His silence is just His silence. Never mistake His silence for detachment. He is never aloof and unresponsive. His silence is often a means to draw us into meditation, which becomes the prelude to worship and the entrance of revelation that then brings change to us. What changes us the most is the unchangeableness of God! Whenever I reflect on the unchangeable nature of God, I want to cry. His constancy and dependability always make me resolve to be like Him. He brings peace to me by His constancy. I feel my heart settling down into Him in the turbulence of situations and events. In crises and conflicts I find myself wanting harmony and love rather than just resolution. To agree to disagree and remain loving friends is a sure sign that God is among us and that we are in love with Him. God is endlessly enthusiastic about people. He has a boundless, unremitting energy. He never stops working, yet He exudes rest and peace. He rests in and through His work. I am never quite sure where my rest in Him gives way to His rest in me. On the seventh day He rested from creating, but He never ceased from maintaining what He had made. It is typical of God that man's first day of creation and life should coincide with God's rest. Our first day began with rest, and a prime part of our relationship with God is to enter His rest. One of my personal goals is to be one of the most restful, peaceful people on the planet. Since I have discovered rest as a major part of my relationship with the Lord, my output has increased significantly. Rest maintains worship, adoration, and focus. It promotes a God-consciousness by the Holy Spirit that increases productivity without detracting from fellowship. The more we rest, the more we get done. Time spent resting brings us into a place where God can do in seconds what we could not do in hours under the anointing. The more we rest, the greater the power to break through. The greater the rest, the more God prepares things around us by His hand. His wisdom increases as we sit and relax in His presence. To rest in the finished work of Calvary is a wonderful privilege. Lack of the presence of God is a major cause of barrenness.

Chapter Ten
The Fire of God's Glory

One of the Characteristics I've seen in God is through the fire of God. The fire of God's glory was manifest as a means of God's directions to the children of Israel.

Exodus 13:21 And the LORD went before them by day in a pillar of a cloud, to lead them the way; and by night in a pillar of fire, to give them light; to go by day and night:

This was a continuous manifestation of God's goodness and glory among His people. Then, when Pharaoh's armies were about to overtake them at the Red Sea, God ordered His angel who was in charge of the pillar of cloud to switch positions and go behind God's people to act as a smoke screen to protect them from their enemies. What a protective God! And He's in business to equally care for His own today, and He hasn't run out of unheard-of ways to do it. In fact, He's the ultimate specialist in that business.

We need to understand that the fire of God's glory can be manifest in both blessing and judgment.

Numbers 16:18 And they took every man his censer, and put fire in them, and laid incense thereon, and stood in the door of the tabernacle of the congregation with Moses and Aaron.

Numbers 16:24 Speak unto the congregation, saying, Get you up from about the tabernacle of Korah, Dathan, and Abiram.

Then God went into action. These four men found themselves with the ground splitting under them and being swallowed up alive as their screams charge the air. Then a fire came out from the Lord and consumed the other 250 rebellious men. We see from this account that the glory of the Lord appearing among the people was a sign that He had showed up, but not with His approving presence. In Numbers 14, we again see the glory of God being manifest at a time we would least expect. After the men had given a bad report to the children of Israel after having spied out the land of Canaan, the people embarked on an all-out murmuring and complaining campaign against Moses and Aaron. The people questioned God's character, suggested returning to Egypt and even proposed selecting another leader in order to do so. Moses and Aaron had their predictable humility reaction by falling on their faces before God as intercessors for the rebellious mob. Joshua and Caleb tore their clothes and gave their version of what the Israelites should do. They exhorted the people not to rebel against the Lord and strongly urged them with encouraging words to not be afraid but to trust and obey God and enter Canaan. The Israelites' reaction was violent. They planned to stone these men of God who had spoken the truth to them.

God talked with Moses, announcing His plan to strike the people with diseases and to disinherit them, while starting over again by making a mightier nation with Moses. God expressed His dismay over the Israelites' rejection of His ruler-ship and unbelief, despite the fact that they had repeatedly witnessed the incredible signs and wonders God had performed on their behalf. Moses' response as an intercessor is unsurpassed in human history, and his boldness can only be explained by the depth and intimacy of his knowledge of God's character. His greatest concern was for God Himself, not the rebellious people he led, and certainly not himself.

Philippians 2:13 For it is God which worketh in you both to will and to do of *his* good pleasure.

The closer the friendship the more understanding of that person's character. God's response to His close friend was in the classic words, *"I have pardoned according to your word"*. God goes on to make this amazing statement. *"But truly as I live, all the earth shall be filled with the glory of the Lord."* I believe God is making the point that despite how humanity messes up on God's intended plans for them, there will come a day when God will display His complete glory by a show of all His characteristics.

His name and character will be totally vindicated in Heaven and earth and under the earth. That's when every knee shall bow and every tongue will confess that Jesus Christ is Lord to the glory of God the Father. Finally, God displays His justice and judgment alongside His compassion and mercy by pronouncing that all those who rejected His ruler-ship would die in the wilderness over the course of their lifespan and not enter Canaan, while all those 20 years old and under would enter as promised.

While God can extend mercy to us by our not getting what we deserve, we must always remember that we will reap what we sow. It is a spiritual law. Sin has its consequences. At the same time, to the depth and extent of our repentance and humbling ourselves, the sentence of reaping will be shortened.

Micah 7:18, 19 Who *is* a God like unto thee, that pardoneth iniquity, and passeth by the transgression of the remnant of his heritage? he retaineth not his anger for ever, because he delighteth *in* mercy. He will turn again, he will have compassion upon us; he will subdue our iniquities; and thou wilt cast all their sins into the depths of the sea.

The fire of God's glory can be so awesome in its intensity that it can be overwhelming. The fire of God, the glory of God, and the power of God are closely linked. And the combination can be unbearably intense.

2 Chronicles 7:1-3 Now when Solomon had made an end of praying, the fire came down from heaven, and consumed the burnt offering and the sacrifices; and the glory of the LORD filled the house. And the priests could not enter into the house of the LORD, because the glory of the LORD had filled the LORD'S house. And when all the children of Israel saw how the fire came down, and the glory of the LORD upon the house, they bowed themselves with their faces to the ground upon the pavement, and worshipped, and praised the LORD, *saying,* For *he is* good; for his mercy *endureth* for ever.

Isaiah 2:5 O house of Jacob, come ye, and let us walk in the light of the LORD.

That simply means to live according to God's standard of holiness found in His Word. He then exposes the sins of idolatry that are manifest through materialism. Throughout this section there are seven strong references to God's actions in humbling everyone who is proud. Pride is always the cause of all idolatry everything that we place of importance more than an ardent pursuit of God Himself.

Isaiah 2:11 The lofty looks of man shall be humbled, and the haughtiness of men shall be bowed down, and the LORD alone shall be exalted in that day.

Isaiah 2:17 And the loftiness of man shall be bowed down, and the haughtiness of men shall be made low: and the LORD alone shall be exalted in that day.

That's God's radical, revolutionary uprising against man's greatest sin!

Isaiah 2:10 Enter into the rock, and hide thee in the dust, for fear of the LORD, and for the glory of his majesty.

Isaiah 2:19 And they shall go into the holes of the rocks, and into the caves of the earth, for fear of the LORD, and for the glory of his majesty, when he ariseth to shake terribly the earth.

Isaiah 2:21 To go into the clefts of the rocks, and into the tops of the ragged rocks, for fear of the LORD, and for the glory of his majesty, when he ariseth to shake terribly the earth.

Unfortunately, we all too seldom hear Bible teaching on these aspects of the fire of God's glory, highlighting the fact that one of our greatest needs is a far greater understanding of God's character and ways.

Psalms 104:4 Who maketh his angels spirits; his ministers a flaming fire:

Job 36:26 Behold, God *is* great, and we know *him* not, neither can the number of his years be searched out.

Job 26:14 Lo, these *are* parts of his ways: but how little a portion is heard of him? but the thunder of his power who can understand?

If we want to be trusted with the fire of God's glory through us, we will have to subjected to the same fire to burn out everything that is not Christ-like.

Chapter Eleven
Transformed Mind

We all have a battlefield of the mind. We need to allow God to transform our minds for a life of freedom. Satan is very much aware of the power of the transformed mind and constantly assaults our minds, which are his greatest battlefields. Whoever wins the battle for our minds is whose servants we'll become. Paul commanded us to think on virtuous things. We cannot allow our minds to dwell upon evil or things that are incompatible with God and expect to be compatible with Him.

1 Corinthians 15:33 Be not deceived: evil communications corrupt good manners.

We have within us the ability to renew our minds and be transformed. The mind is impressionable. We operate in that capacity either consciously or unconsciously. Thoughts are seeds. When thoughts are connected with strong emotion, they become seeds and conception takes place. If that seed is nurtured and incubated, it will reproduce according to the particular framework of that particular pattern of thought, whether for evil or for good. Seed thoughts will manifest and come to pass! One of the most important laws of the Kingdom is that all things reproduce after their own likeness and kind. Your thoughts will reproduce after their own kind.

The minds of people are difficult to understand. The brain is an incredible bioelectric, magnetic mass of gray matter and works similar to a computer. We use our brains to think, to analyze and distribute information, and to arrive at conclusions. Although a computer cannot originate thought, it is programmable. The mind is programmable too. It can be programmed with ideas, concepts, knowledge, and values and will run according to its programming. Satan wants to program your mind to run according to his program with lies and values that are contrary to God's thoughts and ways. Just watch some television for a while and see how many anti-God concepts vie for mind space.

Satan knows that if he can capture your mind your thinking will be out of kilter and then the whole person will be off. When your mind is single, your eye will be single, and your whole body will be full of light. When your mind is free and clean, the doorway is open for God's love and light to flow in and through you. We all need to get our thought lives aligned with the purposes of God and His Word and understand the way that He thinks.

The good news is that God sent us an instruction manual that explains the marvel of the mind and how to use it. That book is the Bible, and it reveals valuable keys to the right and proper use of the mind. It explains why we're incapable, in and of ourselves, of working out His purpose without His divine intervention.

When thoughts and emotions blend, a creative process of birthing starts in the thought life and in the realm of the imagination Satan knows this, so the battle is for who controls your mind. The mind is a receptor and open to spiritual influences, both light and dark

Matthew 6:23 But if thine eye be evil, thy whole body shall be full of darkness. If therefore the light that is in thee be darkness, how great *is* that darkness!

Dark light is the belief that something is true when in actuality it is not. This is deception. The inference is to be careful of the thing you believe to be light, when indeed it is dark Why? Because the mind is the gateway and connector to all incoming spiritual communication.

God designed the mind to act as an internal processor capable of receiving programmable information that could be programmed into the system. Whoever programs your mind will determine the way you think and how your life evolves what your life will become, or your destiny. For within your mind is the foundation of what you really believe about what you believe and the associated emotions that stem from and reinforce the choices you make. Satan will try to win the right to your mind so that he can program it just the way he wants.

God created the human spirit with the ability to receive inspired supernatural information directly from Him and with the capacity to direct and influence the mind, will, emotions, and flesh to manifest in the natural what we receive from Him in the spirit. Consider that God is Spirit, and He created humankind with the very breath of His Spirit. Humans, as spirit, have the capacity to create and originate thought. This is the wonderful and powerful dimension from which all miracles, signs, and wonders come that manifest from the realm of Glory.

On earth, humans are the only created beings that possess a spirit, intellect, and reason. We also have thoughts, emotions, and behaviors unique to us as spirit beings created in the image of God. Humans are capable of loving God; the inferior creatures are not.

Psalms 139:14 I will praise thee; for I am fearfully *and* wonderfully made: marvellous *are* thy works; and *that* my soul knoweth right well.

This is true of your brain. It is amazing, but it is also incomplete in that we must constantly acquire physical and spiritual knowledge.

We gain physical knowledge with our five senses We see, hear, smell, touch, and taste and constantly add to our knowledge base. We gain spiritual knowledge in a similar way by developing and using our spiritual senses. When we draw close to God and allow God to strengthen, teach, and lead us through and by His Spirit, spiritual desires spring forth and we accomplish spiritual things. With a Spirit-led mind, we will find the way into that supernatural realm of God's Kingdom and all of its treasures. If we can spiritually see God's Kingdom, how much more will we desire it? The spirit of humankind was designed by God to receive knowledge and understanding. We call this revelation. With it we decipher information from the physical world with our five senses, and we can see, touch, smell, hear, and taste things from the spiritual realm by God's Spirit. Each of us has the privilege and awesome responsibility of programming our own brain, and we will live according to this programming.

Proverbs 22:6 Train up a child in the way he should go: and when he is old, he will not depart from it.

What we program into the life of a child may govern his or her life in adulthood. What we program into our minds will govern our lives. If we program our children right when they are young, they won't depart from it when they are old. A child may deviate from the program from time to time, but eventually he or she will "run" according to the programming. Sometimes we end up with wrong programming that runs contrary to the design of God; however, when we are born again, we are supernaturally infused with the holy seed of God. In that very seed is all of who God is. In time, with the proper care from the Holy Spirit and the Word, that seed will grow and bear the exact likeness and makeup of the original Seed. Contained in the seed is all of who God is spiritually and the very likeness and image of Christ Jesus.

2 Timothy 3:15 And that from a child thou hast known the holy scriptures, which are able to make thee wise unto salvation through faith which is in Christ Jesus.

Philippians 1:27 Only let your conversation be as it becometh the gospel of Christ: that whether I come and see you, or else be absent, I may hear of your affairs, that ye stand fast in one spirit, with one mind striving together for the faith of the gospel;

Light will flow into your being and the transformation process will begin when there's harmony between your mind and your spirit. Harmony comes through freedom from blockages, renewal, and reprogramming of the mind. If your mind runs against the truth, the Seed in your spirit cannot grow. Cast out everything that is not the truth of God's Word, and the truth will renew your mind and you'll see rapid growth in your life. Quickened truth is when revelation comes and you receive it. Revelation carries with it the power to renew your mind.

1 Corinthians 2:16 For who hath known the mind of the Lord, that he may instruct him? But we have the mind of Christ.

Your mind is the gateway between the spirit and physical realm for the whole person, so your mind and spirit must agree. When you were born again your spirit and mind were no longer compatible, so it's an ongoing process to reprogram the mind to conform to the mind of Christ in your spirit. Deposited in your spirit person is the mind of Christ. Yes, your spirit has a mind the mind of Christ!

Ephesians 4:23 And be renewed in the spirit of your mind;

Your mind can originate thought as part of the creative process. However, it can also be inspired by your spirit and the Holy Spirit within you; for example, when you instantly get a spark of revelation or a knowing of something you hadn't known previously. This will occur more and more frequently as your mind is renewed and becomes submissive to your spirit. They must be in harmony or there will be blockages. The brain will sift and sort information it receives, but unless that harmony exists with the spirit, the un-renewed mind will toss out supernatural revelation or block it altogether.

1 Corinthians 2:14 But the natural man receiveth not the things of the Spirit of God: for they are foolishness unto him: neither can he know *them*, because they are spiritually discerned.

The natural mind is the mind or the soul life programmed with the concepts of this world and the kingdom of darkness. The spiritual person must be programmed with different thinking.

1 Corinthians 2:12 Now we have received, not the spirit of the world, but the spirit which is of God; that we might know the things that are freely given to us of God.

1 Corinthians 6:17 But he that is joined unto the Lord is one spirit.

Your spirit has become one with the Lord Everything that God is already lives in your spirit person. We are joined to the Lord and are one spirit with Him. We must align the brain with the spirit bringing the brain and spirit into unity so that they are not running on separate programs.

Romans 12:2 And be not conformed to this world: but be ye transformed by the renewing of your mind, that ye may prove what *is* that good, and acceptable, and perfect, will of God.

Your brain has to be transformed from the soulish concepts of the world by the Word of God, which you receive whether you understand it or not. There are many things in the Word of God that we have yet to understand. We read things and pass them by because there is a layer there that is not coming through to us. God's Word is truth whether we understand it or not. And it starts with this we accept God's Word whether we understand it or not. It is God's Word. This is the first step in renewal. The greatest hindrance to walking with God is the un-renewed brain.

Philippians 4:8 Finally, brethren, whatsoever things are true, whatsoever things *are* honest, whatsoever things *are* just, whatsoever things *are* pure, whatsoever things *are* lovely, whatsoever things *are* of good report; if *there be* any virtue, and if *there be* any praise, think on these things.

This Scripture should guard our minds at all times. It should act as a filter that we place over our mind. If it is not true, honest, or pure, reject it.

Romans 8:7 Because the carnal mind *is* enmity against God: for it is not subject to the law of God, neither indeed can be.

In other words, the natural mind is an enemy of God. This statement provides startling insight into the workings of the carnal, natural mind. When the mind is cut off from God, the mind is an enemy of God the mind hates Him. Your spirit may be born again, but if your mind is un-renewed there is conflict. Your spirit flows through the mind and truth is blocked or corrupted and altered because of wrong concepts. If we can get our thinking patterns renewed to be compatible with our spirit man, there will be a unity that will open a supernatural gateway from Heaven that will allow light, understanding, and knowledge to flow into our being and transform us. It is then that we will understand the mysteries of creation and the universe. We will understand God and the purposes of God because our brains will be in harmony with Him. The supernatural pathways only open when the two become compatible.

Your spirit came from Heaven and has been in existence for a long time I am talking spirit here, not the soul. The soul is what each person is as a human being A person cannot exist outside of the soul.

It is important that we as spirit, soul, and body blend as one so we can interact with the spiritual realm and the physical realm. Heaven was first a spiritual world. But God created the earth and brought Heaven to earth, bringing it into a physical dimension. When you were born again Christ came into your spirit. That seed is more than just spirit. You are a living soul and the mind is the key. In a previous chapter, we talked about living and moving by the Law of the Spirit.

Demons or evil spirits can lodge over the brain to control or influence the pathways of thinking and corrupt the imagination. They filter any pure light of revelation coming to us. When this happens, a person needs deliverance. The demonic spirit realm can and does influence us, and if we allow it entry it may attach itself to our thought life or our imagination, creating a spiritual stronghold. Evil spirits build strongholds, and they attach themselves to us as a false concept or way of thinking. They clothe our minds, projecting unclean thoughts into our thinking, strengthening untruths. If we refuse them the doors or pathways will close. The more we close the doors, the better; they will eventually give up. We have to be diligent door-closers because the spirits have an incredible capacity to interact with the brain as they project pictures, thoughts, or concepts. If we do not slam the door shut they may nest in our minds and even multiply.

Our dreams and vision must be in line with what God has called us to and what our future is. If we can start to get even a small amount of compatibility between our spirit and our brain, we will start to fill up with light. We will see the wonders of God. We will begin to understand like never before. The creative side of our life will begin to blossom, and we will begin to flow into our destiny. Many people have a destiny and never fulfill it because they can't see it and don't believe it. Their minds are not big enough to accommodate their destiny. The spirit is certainly big enough, but the brain is limited.

God will have a supernatural people, a Glory generation in these last days that will do great things that we have never thought possible. We have to be changed now we have to become the overcoming Body of Christ if we with Christ will rule the world. We have to align our mind and spirit if we're to do the "all things are possible." We can have such an impact on the Glory harvest when we enlarge our thinking by aligning it with our spirit. Going to church every Sunday will not do it, but having Heaven's mind will.

The battlefield is in the mind. We have a fierce adversary who wants control of it. How do we take it back? Our lives have to become so transparent that people see Jesus through our life experiences and actions.

All that Jesus did in a single body He will do again through the corporate Body as an end-time witness to the nations, giving some to be apostles, some prophets, some evangelists, and some pastors and teachers for the work of the ministry. Through an act of intervention, we are about to be lifted into the spirit realm, where ministry will function through relationship rather than through gifting. There we'll find straight paths to the hidden riches of secret places.

Isaiah 45:1-3 Thus saith the LORD to his anointed, to Cyrus, whose right hand I have holden, to subdue nations before him; and I will loose the loins of kings, to open before him the two leaved gates; and the gates shall not be shut; I will go before thee, and make the crooked places straight: I will break in pieces the gates of brass, and cut in sunder the bars of iron: And I will give thee the treasures of darkness, and hidden riches of secret places, that thou mayest know that I, the LORD, which call *thee* by thy name, *am* the God of Israel.

Jesus knew all about straight paths. He could and did walk through walls. As we mature in sonship, renewing our minds for transformation, we too will have the ability to seamlessly walk in the seemingly impossible. We can breach walls of resistance and walls built to keep us out. When we come through them to the other side, we won't know how we got there, just as Peter didn't understand how he was able to walk on water, because walking in the ways of the law of the Spirit defies all natural reasoning. To those walking with the wind of the Spirit, to those walking in the power of a transformed mind, to those walking in compatibility with God as co-heirs, God says the gates shall not be shut. These spiritual gates open wide to the spiritual sons and daughters of God who will find access into Eden's door and to the Tree of Life. They are destiny's double doors that will open for you to encounter God in genuine, tangible ways, executing and partaking of the ever-increasing and all-powerful realm of Glory in the Kingdom of God for His Glory. Are you ready to break into new dimensions of the realities of the Glory realm of God?

Chapter Twelve
A New Level

God is releasing a greater level of healings, miracles, signs and wonders. I believe that if we're to continue to see miracles, signs and wonders today, we need to operate in a spirit of counsel; this will release God's might and power.

God's power is always connected to wisdom, knowledge and revelation. The word of knowledge is a God-given tool that empowers the healing ministry.

I saw in the Spirit that it's as if God has reserved this mountain high place for Himself and will gather ministries together. This is happening all over the World. Days of experiences with the Lord Jesus - visitations of the Lord, trances, dreams, and hearing God intimately while we lie on the carpet are coming!

For many years I've desired to walk in the supernatural. When I got awaken, I was extremely hungry to walk in the Spirit. I read that Elisha had eyes to see into the heavens and he prayed that the eyes of his servant Gehazi would be opened so that Gehazi could see into the heavens. Then they both saw into the second heaven; they saw angels and they saw demons.

I want to know what my Father is doing in heaven before he does it. I want the ministry of Jesus. Even in ministry today, it's so important that we operate in that gift especially in the area of healing. We need to come into a place where we know what God is going to do before he does it because we've already seen it.

Ephesians 1:17 That the God of our Lord Jesus Christ, the Father of glory, may give unto you the spirit of wisdom and revelation in the knowledge of him:

Quite often before a meeting I just lay before the Lord and I'd say, Let me see that meeting God. What will the altar call look like? When does it happen? The Word of knowledge flows because I took the time to see what my Father was doing. I spoke out what he was doing and he did it. It had nothing to do with me, except that I took the time to get counsel. God describes the details of the word of knowledge that accurately described his situation. With no laying on of hands, just the spoken word, he says, people were completely healed. The word of knowledge is such a powerful tool.

In Ephesians 1:17 the Apostle Paul prays that: "...the God of our Lord Jesus Christ, the Father of glory may give to you the spirit of wisdom and revelation in the knowledge of Him". It is not just the knowledge of him that God wants to give us; it is the knowledge of what he is doing as well. In verse 18 Paul continues to pray that the eyes of the hearts' of God's people would be enlightened that they would know the hope of His calling and the surpassing greatness of his power. He then adds that all this knowledge and revelation is in accordance with the working of the strength of God's might that he brought about in Christ when he raised him from the dead. You'll notice in this passage there's a connection between wisdom and knowledge and the exceeding greatness of his power. The apostle Paul is saying that God wants us to have a revelation of the exceeding greatness of his power towards us who believe. Why? So we can know that the same Spirit that raised Christ from the dead lives in us.

You can know in your mind that you are a temple of the Holy Ghost and that the God of the universe dwells in you. You can know Christ in you, the hope of glory, but you're still not going to walk in the demonstration of that power until you get beyond the logos to the rhema (quickened personal word). It's in the rhema of God that we find the exceeding greatness of his power.

What the Holy Spirit does is always connected to counsel. It's the Spirit of counsel and the Spirit of might; the might is always connected to the wisdom and the realm of knowledge that's where God's power is. We're only to do those things we see the Father doing and speak those things we hear the Father saying that's where the power, miracles, healings, signs and wonders are. Remember, by his stripes we are healed. This truth blows the minds of many Christians because it's not a quickened rhema word to them. They have a hard time receiving healing now because they haven't seen everybody healed, even though they may believe that God wants to heal all. I believe that there's a place where healing jumps out of eternity, out of the future, and it comes on you in the present. That's why it's so important that we understand the word of knowledge in the area of ministering healing. It's not that God's word isn't God's word, but that we don't yet have a heart revelation of it. Christians who don't understand the importance of revelation often take dry scriptural truths, speak them outside of the timing of the Lord and bring death instead of life. God wants to give us personal quickened words from heaven. How many times have you opened up a passage of scripture and it was alive to you and you lived in that passage? That passage meant nothing to others, but to you it was a living, powerful truth. Then next month something else jumps off the page and grabs your heart it's your word from the

Lord. I believe God is getting rid of sermons, and he's releasing these messages to people's hearts. He is opening up the realm of knowledge, so it's no longer just speaking what God has already said over 2000 years ago, even though that message is still true. It's still important for the Holy Spirit to be involved in the ministry of the word to our hearts because it's the Spirit that makes it alive and real to us. This alive word is what the word of knowledge is.

In North America today, there is a wasting disease in the souls of Christians because they haven't understood how to wait, receive and operate in the word of knowledge. Many just do whatever they want to and ask God to bless it because they don't have time to seek Him first. While I was in prayer, the Lord warned me to be careful of this tendency for us as believers to depend on our understanding instead of the voice of the Spirit.

God is the Alpha and Omega, the first and the last, the beginning and end, the everlasting Father and the great "I am". He has seen the beginning of time, the end of time and everything in between. Before anyone else was, He was. He is the one who was, who is and who is to come. There's never been anybody before Him or after Him He is God.

God wants to give us these glimpses into the future because He has things that he has purposed and predestined in eternity before the foundation of the world. All I have to do is get into those heavenly places and invite the Holy Spirit to breathe on me with His Spirit of wisdom, revelation, understanding, counsel and might.

Chapter Thirteen
The Key to the Nation

In the new prototype Church God is giving us keys to the Nations. This is a new level of power and authority being released.

Isaiah 11:2 And the spirit of the LORD shall rest upon him, the spirit of wisdom and understanding, the spirit of counsel and might, the spirit of knowledge and of the fear of the LORD;

In this scripture we're seeing wisdom, knowledge, understanding and the Spirit of counsel and might God's counsel releases might. The wonderful counselor releases power, signs and wonders. It doesn't matter if you have enough faith or anointing or whether somebody lays hands on you or not. When you're operating in the realm of knowledge, it's no longer about you, but it's about everything the Father has already done in his purpose. When you begin to take time to listen for the Father's directions and hear his purposes, then you can begin to speak them out with authority. Then he does what he said he would do, because you've seen what he wanted to do. You take the blueprint of what God has already said in heaven and you act on it. It's like Moses he just built what he already saw in heaven.

Abraham was also a man of God who knew about the Father's purposes. God told Abraham to leave his country and go to a land that He would show him. He would show him a city, who's builder and maker is God. Yes, the Lord is going to build this thing, and He's going to give us the blueprint. When we operate in the purposes of God it's so important to do it exactly the way we saw God do it.

When we don't take time to wait on the Lord for His purposes in ministry, it abuses the people of God. It doesn't feed the spirits of the people of God, because we're not operating on the rhema word, the quickened word. The Bible also tells us that man shall not live by bread alone but by every word that proceeds out of the mouth of God. There is still a proceeding word; power is in that word and rest is in that word. When we receive that word we cease from our labors and enter into the purposes of God.

Psalms 106:13-15 They soon forgat his works; they waited not for his counsel: But lusted exceedingly in the wilderness, and tempted God in the desert. And he gave them their request; but sent leanness into their soul.

That verse actually means he sent leanness into their soul. God put leanness into their soul because they did not wait for his counsel. They did not take time to really hear God. They really didn't believe that the Father wanted to speak to them and that his sheep hear his voice. In the book of Revelation God put a wasting in their soul and there was a famine.

Just as in that time, I tell you, there is a famine in the land today in North America. There is a wasting disease in the soul of the North American church, because we now have programs, and seeker-friendly events. Now we have all the religion and all the form of godliness but we deny the power. We've got all the Mega-churches, we've got all the professional preachers and all those who are politically correct. We've got all those who think they are something because they've got a degree. We've got all the professional music, all the big carpets and the big million-dollar buildings. We've got all the things we think we need to do the ministry of Jesus and it looks real good. We've got all the tools, but we're empty and nobody's getting saved, healed or delivered. We don't see a whole lot of power except for every once in a while when a healing evangelist comes in to minister.

Ephesians 1:20 Which he wrought in Christ, when he raised him from the dead, and set *him* at his own right hand in the heavenly *places,*

Our religious mindset thinks it's a particular group of people a denomination or a particular stream. That Scripture tells us, we as believers are the fullness of him, the fullness of the Godhead in bodily form. We can live in that fullness just like Jesus who had the spirit without measure.

In Ephesians, even though the apostle Paul was talking to Spirit-filled believers, he was saying to them, "You're still not operating in the fullness of what God has for you". He was saying to them that they hadn't really wanted the Spirit without measure because they've been satisfied and have limited God in their mindset. They hadn't really been hungry and desperate and they hadn't really understood that God wants them to be ministers of power just as much as the pastor. The Lord wants believers to realize that it's impossible for us to walk in the power.

Ephesians 1:19 And what *is* the exceeding greatness of his power to us-ward who believe, according to the working of his mighty power,

Like the Ephesians church, we need to realize that it's not just about the apostles, prophets, teachers, evangelists and those that God is raising up in the five-fold ministry. When the Holy Spirit started revealing this to me, He asked: "Do you know what the church needs to look like in North America? It needs to look like an expression of who I was 2000 years ago. And more than anything, who I was, was seeking and saving the lost. When you saw me in scripture, you saw the gospel preached, the sick and diseased healed and those oppressed of the devil set free."

Chapter Fourteen
Living in the Fire

I Think now would be a good time to talk more about the Fire of God. Now this is going to be a bit different. To live in the Fire of God is making it through the good times and the burning purifying fire. We will learn how to react to the different aspects of the fire of God.

Isaiah 43:2 When thou passest through the waters, I *will be* with thee; and through the rivers, they shall not overflow thee: when thou walkest through the fire, thou shalt not be burned; neither shall the flame kindle upon thee.

God has promised that when we walk through the fire we shall not be burned, nor shall the flame scorch us. The following truths give understanding how that promise can be fulfilled. The longer God keeps us in the fire and the hotter the flames; these are the attributes of God we'll be most tempted to doubt. When God allows us to be stripped of everything, and there's absolutely nothing left for us to depend on but His character, we had better have in-depth revelation, because in the greatest heat of the fiery trial, God can purposely withdraw all other understanding. My faith may have wavered had I not taken much time to study God's character as a way of life. I had nothing left to cling to, or hang my faith on, when in the furnace of affliction and we can be so ill, we're incapable of discerning His voice. Perplexing and discouraging circumstances have been frequent and continual.

2 Corinthians 4:8 *We are* troubled on every side, yet not distressed; *we are* perplexed, but not in despair;

Romans 11:33 O the depth of the riches both of the wisdom and knowledge of God! how unsearchable *are* his judgments, and his ways past finding out!

We are warned in God's Word that if we try to take matters into our own hands, by forming our own conclusions and making our own decisions when we are in confusing situations, we will land in big trouble.

Isaiah 50:10, 11 Who *is* among you that feareth the LORD, that obeyeth the voice of his servant, that walketh *in* darkness, and hath no light? let him trust in the name of the LORD, and stay upon his God. Behold, all ye that kindle a fire, that compass *yourselves* about with sparks: walk in the light of your fire, and in the sparks *that* ye have kindled. This shall ye have of mine hand; ye shall lie down in sorrow.

It always pays to keep trusting God's unwavering faithfulness, infinite wisdom and knowledge, absolute justice and unfathomable love, no matter how dark and perplexing the circumstances.

Hebrews 12:2 Looking unto Jesus the author and finisher of *our* faith; who for the joy that was set before him endured the cross, despising the shame, and is set down at the right hand of the throne of God.

We are Christ-centered in direct proportion to how automatically we relate our everyday circumstances to the Lord Jesus Christ.

Psalms 16:8, 9 I have set the LORD always before me: because *he is* at my right hand, I shall not be moved. Therefore my heart is glad, and my glory rejoiceth: my flesh also shall rest in hope.

Psalms 34:1 ***A Psalm* of David, when he changed his behaviour before Abimelech; who drove him away, and he departed.** I will bless the LORD at all times: his praise *shall* continually *be* in my mouth.

It will not only keep our focus and perspective right, but it may well keep our sanity, it did mine. It's also a powerful means of spiritual warfare.

Ephesians 6:10-18 Finally, my brethren, be strong in the Lord, and in the power of his might. Put on the whole armour of God, that ye may be able to stand against the wiles of the devil. For we wrestle not against flesh and blood, but against principalities, against powers, against the rulers of the darkness of this world, against spiritual wickedness in high *places*. Wherefore take unto you the whole armour of God, that ye may be able to withstand in the evil day, and having done all, to stand. Stand therefore, having your loins girt about with truth, and having on the breastplate of righteousness; And your feet shod with the preparation of the gospel of peace; Above all, taking the shield of faith, wherewith ye shall be able to quench all the fiery darts of the wicked. And take the helmet of salvation, and the sword of the Spirit, which is the word of God: Praying always with all prayer and supplication in the Spirit, and watching thereunto with all perseverance and supplication for all saints;

Either the devil is harassing us, or we're harassing him. Be on the offensive daily, and resist him in Jesus' name before he can attack us.

1 Peter 5:8, 9 Be sober, be vigilant; because your adversary the devil, as a roaring lion, walketh about, seeking whom he may devour: Whom resist stedfast in the faith, knowing that the same afflictions are accomplished in your brethren that are in the world.

When we walk in the fear of the Lord, we don't fear devils. They fear us. It's the only pathway to fulfillment and blessing.

If we think we can, then God may well make it hotter until we know we can't. So decide now to be open to declare your weakness and call for help. Jesus did, three times in the garden of Gethsemane. He asked for prayer support from some of His closest friends when He was facing the agonies of being separated from His Father during the times of His greatest need. This included becoming sin for all sinners, while enduring the excruciating pain of crucifixion.

Be encouraged and be glad that we'll come through the fire in better shape than when we went in, if we cooperate with God's purposes. Parallel to that, we'll find ourselves seeking Him diligently for more understanding, and doing our best to believe His many promises for deliverance and healing.

Psalms 34:19 Many *are* the afflictions of the righteous: but the LORD delivereth him out of them all.

We keep seeking God for greater understanding of His character and ways and anything He wants to say to us. When He speaks, we obey. We never limit Him through unbelief. At the same time we rest in His flawless character, and trust Him to perfect that which concerns us.

Don't let God go. Persist until He speaks to you personally in your fire. Write it down, believe it, and hang on to it in faith and declare it back to God. We can also ask God to send us specific Rhema words from Himself through reliable, trusted sources as well, for confirmation.

You'll see Him sovereignly adjust the temperature according to His divine purpose, not because He's capricious. He's revealing to you that He understands your circumstances. He's in control. I have witnessed this truth on numerous occasions, and when the pain has sovereignly and temporarily lifted I have always seen God's purposes in doing so. It's been truly remarkable.

Are we willing to wait for the timing that will bring the greatest glory to His name? Even if that means our circumstances may get worse, as well as be prolonged? Can we trust God's character to that degree? We can be thankful for learning so much about our amazing God who is a consuming fire of holiness and love. We'll have come to discover that the power of the Lord Jesus' person, presence, and purposes during the fire are stronger than the heat of the flames. This should produce more of a burning and passionate love for Him, which, in turn, motivates us to qualify for the promises.

Revelations 2:26 And he that overcometh, and keepeth my works unto the end, to him will I give power over the nations:

Our choice to live this message determines not only our destiny here on earth but what God can trust us with in the ages to come.

Chapter Fifteen
Wealth of the Nations

We are entering a year of plenty. I am not talking about a calendar year but a spiritual season of blessings.

The Holy Spirit will give me something fresh each year to believe for a higher level so I can be focused on where the blessing will be. Here is what I have heard as a key theme for the coming year.

We want to have a faith level for this year.

Isaiah 60:11 Therefore thy gates shall be open continually; they shall not be shut day nor night; that *men* may bring unto thee the forces of the Gentiles, and *that* their kings *may be* brought.

Can you imagine this in your business, ministry or church? The gates or doors are open twenty four hours a day for continual receiving! The wealth just keeps coming. Why? What is the key to stepping into the kind of wealth the Lord is releasing now?

A key chapter is Isaiah 60

There are three major themes in this chapter:

1. Harvest and Prodigals

2. Glory Presence

3. Financial wealth

Isaiah 60:1 Arise, shine; for thy light is come, and the glory of the LORD is risen upon thee.

It is time to Arise and shine!

Isaiah 60:2 For, behold, the darkness shall cover the earth, and gross darkness the people: but the LORD shall arise upon thee, and his glory shall be seen upon thee.

What is the King of Glory?

Glory = Chabod (kah-vohd) Strongs: 3519: weightiness: that which is substantial or heavy, glory, honor, splendor, power, wealth, riches, authority, dignity, visible splendor and substance.

Isaiah 60:3, 4 And the Gentiles shall come to thy light, and kings to the brightness of thy rising. Lift up thine eyes round about, and see: all they gather themselves together, they come to thee: thy sons shall come from far, and thy daughters shall be nursed at *thy* side.

The prodigals are coming home. Wealth of the Nations Simultaneously during the great harvest in the nations, when we arise and shine we will see a release of great provision. Remember what the glory presence is.

Isaiah 60:5, 6 Then thou shalt see, and flow together, and thine heart shall fear, and be enlarged; because the abundance of the sea shall be converted unto thee, the forces of the Gentiles shall come unto thee. The multitude of camels shall cover thee, the dromedaries of Midian and Ephah; all they from Sheba shall come: they shall bring gold and incense; and they shall shew forth the praises of the LORD.

God is going to release unprecedented wealth for those who say yes. We know this is a time of the Joseph's anointing. We must store up in the years of plenty for the famine that is coming.

There are billions of dollars in illegal sex, pornography, drugs, child labor, prostitution, organized crime and more. It is time for the wealth of the sinner to be turned to the just. God will bless the church with more wealth than we need to do what he has called us to do. God will release this financial favor on those who Arise and Shine! There is a release of a spirit of wisdom and revelation to prosper. What to do, when, where and how.

God spoke to me that we were not growing at the pace the Lord had for us fully and our wineskin, infrastructures and thinking big levels would not be able to contain what the Lord has for us coming in the year. One thing that will keep us from the wealth is thinking to small. I can't help but believe with the purpose of that is also a focus for the year for many Ministries. Of course with the receiving of great wealth comes great responsibility. At the end of Acts 4 we see money from lands and houses laid at the feet of the apostles to distribute to the poor and widows. That is what the wealth is for. Then in Acts 5 the first few verses we have the fear of the Lord factor with Ananias and Sapphira. It was a call to a higher standard of responsibility, faithfulness and holiness.

Psalms 2:8 Ask of me, and I shall give *thee* the heathen *for* thine inheritance, and the uttermost parts of the earth *for* thy possession.

Revelations 11:15 And the seventh angel sounded; and there were great voices in heaven, saying, The kingdoms of this world are become *the kingdoms* of our Lord, and of his Christ; and he shall reign for ever and ever.

Psalms 24:1 **A Psalm of David.** The earth *is* the LORD'S, and the fulness thereof; the world, and they that dwell therein.

Can a nation be saved in a day? What kind of a harvest perspective do we have? How easy is it for God to do the impossible?

Time and resources spent on the harvest will only bring us into the rest of Isaiah 60.

Isaiah 60:7-11 All the flocks of Kedar shall be gathered together unto thee, the rams of Nebaioth shall minister unto thee: they shall come up with acceptance on mine altar, and I will glorify the house of my glory. Who *are* these *that* fly as a cloud, and as the doves to their windows? Surely the isles shall wait for me, and the ships of Tarshish first, to bring thy sons from far, their silver and their gold with them, unto the name of the LORD thy God, and to the Holy One of Israel, because he hath glorified thee. And the sons of strangers shall build up thy walls, and their kings shall minister unto thee: for in my wrath I smote thee, but in my favour have I had mercy on thee. Therefore thy gates shall be open continually; they shall not be shut day nor night; that *men* may bring unto thee the forces of the Gentiles, and *that* their kings *may be* brought.

Chapter Sixteen
AWARENESS of God

When I was preaching at the Waves of Revival in Belleville, IL; I taught a message on this AWARENESS of God. This is going to release a greater sensitivity of God. As we carry on in the faith, holding to our belief systems and trusting God will move in and through us along the way, I would like to put things on pause for a moment.

Life is one continuous flow for us as the moments, sometimes hours go by without a trace of awareness of what we are to be experiencing in God. Every second of every minute of every hour of every day of every week of every month of every year we are made in God's image and created to function as one with Him at all times and in all situations, ever conscious of God in us, ever aware of this oneness.

John 17:10, 11 And all mine are thine, and thine are mine; and I am glorified in them. And now I am no more in the world, but these are in the world, and I come to thee. Holy Father, keep through thine own name those whom thou hast given me, that they may be one, as we *are*.

John 17:20-22 Neither pray I for these alone, but for them also which shall believe on me through their word; That they all may be one; as thou, Father, *art* in me, and I in thee, that they also may be one in us: that the world may believe that thou hast sent me. And the glory which thou gavest me I have given them; that they may be one, even as we are one:

There is a never ending flow in us that comes from the very essence of who He is as we accept Him as our personal Savior and live out our lives, filled with His Spirit. We are so tied into the physical aspect of who we are that it's difficult for us to wrap our minds around the fact that we are first and foremost a spiritual being, made in God's image, encased in this temporal physical manifestation. The fact that we live this life in a physical body throws off our perspective because it results in our having such a strong mindset toward the physical realm. But did you know that you as a physical being actually flicker in and out of time and space millions of times per second? It's not so as you would notice because it happens so rapidly that our natural eye is unable to distinguish it. It's a scientific fact that our being is an energy flow that manifests in a physical way, just as does the bed you lay on, the table you sit at, the chair you sit on - everything.

This world we live in is held together by God's awareness of all things, in all of creation, at all times! Amazing! It's astonishing what science is discovering that redefines our perspective of our existence. And yet, as Christians, we should be excited that what is being revealed through all of these studies is all found in the Word!

2 Corinthians 4:18 While we look not at the things which are seen, but at the things which are not seen: for the things which are seen *are* temporal; but the things which are not seen *are* eternal.

Colossians 1:17 And he is before all things, and by him all things consist.

Science has been discovering the mysteries of the gospel and unfolding them to us, if we have an ear to hear, especially in these last few decades. One such discovery has to do with the fact that we are energy. As energy we are much more pliable and have much more influence as a created human being than we are aware of.

To the degree that we are aware of who we are in Christ and the dominion we are given we will be effective. How we influence our surroundings and are impacted by them is greatly impacted by our awareness of the interaction between ourselves and the world around us, both physical and spiritual. We must awaken to the fullness of who we are intended to be with a full awareness of the eternal and physical realms at the same time. One foot in each realm, as a spirit being encased in a physical body, yet not limited by its boundaries! God alone is our boundaries and our borders, not this physical realm. We need to live in the full awareness of this as we awaken to the position we hold in Him, both in heavenly places and on the earth. We are seated with Him in heavenly places while we are yet in these mortal bodies on the earth!

Romans 13:11 And that, knowing the time, that now *it is* high time to awake out of sleep: for now *is* our salvation nearer than when we believed.

Ephesians 5:14 Wherefore he saith, Awake thou that sleepest, and arise from the dead, and Christ shall give thee light.

Both of these verses are in the context of coming out of a dullness of mind and spirit so that we do not fall into the complacency of the day, whether it be sin or unbelief. We can no longer afford to live the days, hours and moments on automatic, but must become aware of every present moment in our lives. All we have is this present moment. What is in the past is gone and what is in the future has not yet been, at least that is true of what goes on in our time and space realm. But in every moment we have the endless possibilities of how our lives can change, how our mentalities can shift and our awareness can become stronger and influence not only ourselves, but the world around us.

2 Corinthians 5:16, 17 Wherefore henceforth know we no man after the flesh: yea, though we have known Christ after the flesh, yet now henceforth know we *him* no more. Therefore if any man *be* in Christ, *he is* a new creature: old things are passed away; behold, all things are become new.

Unfortunately, we are still buying into the old. We still believe we are ruled by the limitations set on man between the fall and resurrection of Christ! Let it not be so any longer! We have no idea what an amazing creation we are in Christ and have been living our lives in the deafening dullness of what has been before - the way of the old man! When words are released into our ear, it is nothing but vibrations that we have attached learned meaning to. Air molecules vibrate, sending a signal to the inner ear, which then sends a message to the auditory part of our brain where the message is relayed and affects our whole being. If it is a language we don't understand, we have no awareness of what is being spoken and our body doesn't respond or become aware of what has been relayed. On the other hand, if it is in a language we recognize, we take in that sound with awareness and it influences us for positive or negative, depending on the message. It can cause a reaction at the cellular level as though you just took into your body a drug composed of chemicals! That's how impacting our emotional and spiritual response to things can be on our body, on our whole being. Medicine is just now coming to grips with the reality of how body, mind and soul inter-relate. That is how God created us to interact with each other and our surroundings. That is why he urges us repeatedly in scripture to think on the good, the 'whatsoever things are pure'. Everything we come across leaves some sort of impact. Any two particles that have ever interfaced are connected forever. Science is now learning just how (one) we all are in Christ, in whom all things exist!

Philippians 4:7, 8 And the peace of God, which passeth all understanding, shall keep your hearts and minds through Christ Jesus. Finally, brethren, whatsoever things are true, whatsoever things *are* honest, whatsoever things *are* just, whatsoever things *are* pure, whatsoever things *are* lovely, whatsoever things *are* of good report; if *there be* any virtue, and if *there be* any praise, think on these things.

To be aware every moment of every day of the positive things in ourselves and those around us could drastically change our lives. That is why He urges us repeatedly in scripture to have a grateful heart; So that we can live in that place of abiding love. To be conscious at all times - in this present moment - of the flow of God in us so that we have a constant awareness of our oneness with Him would cause us to view circumstances around us very differently. I wonder if that is not what is behind Paul urging us to pray without ceasing. Perhaps that is why he found it so beneficial to always be praying in tongues to the point that he said I pray in tongues more than ALL of you! It put him in a place of acute awareness of his oneness with God.

Yes, our own awareness of the goodness of God in these days will go a long way to bring us through some challenging circumstances. We will do well to be awakened to the reality of the Spirit realm and the spiritual truths in scripture that can overcome what we are both seeing and not seeing with the natural eye. In doing so, we put on the full armor of God as we wash over our minds and hearts with God's perspective of things.

Does it mean there are no troubles?

Not at all, but we move through them with 'grace grace on our lips and with that same acute awareness at all times of the love and goodness of God that Paul had, loosing miracles to flow through him.

Zechariah 4:6, 7 Then he answered and spake unto me, saying, This *is* the word of the LORD unto Zerubbabel, saying, Not by might, nor by power, but by my spirit, saith the LORD of hosts. Who *art* thou, O great mountain? before Zerubbabel *thou shalt become* a plain: and he shall bring forth the headstone *thereof with* shoutings, *crying,* Grace, grace unto it.

It is time to shift our focus to things that hold eternal value so that we might be ones who will be able to bring healing and deliverance to the masses in this hour. We've heard over and over that the darkness will get darker and the light lighter, but we cannot presume that we will partake of this light if we have not looked into the Light as preparation. We are changed as we behold Him. We need to exercise our spirit man to release strength and clarity of mind as we "set our thoughts on things above."

The Church is in a Season of Profound of Transition

Psalms 17:15 As for me, I will behold thy face in righteousness: I shall be satisfied, when I awake, with thy likeness.

To be ever present with Him is to be aware in every moment that He is in us and we are in Him. Out of that present awareness, that place of oneness, we will see change in ourselves, as well as in the atmosphere around us. We are made in His image, the One Who was and is and is to come!

Churches have become almost mini-seminaries, many having several teaching sessions each week. Where there is no outlet for truth, decay sets in. We become expert listeners, but if our hearing does not progress to the point of our doing, then we are deceived. Deception does not have to be rooted in dishonesty or obvious sinfulness carefully coated with a surface of respectability. Teaching that is not rooted in discipleship has no place to be birthed in the lives of people. The whole point of leadership and ministry is to produce a body of people capable of doing the work. What we have produced from our colleges and schools is a leadership that does everything. Error occurs when truth and practice are not combined. Many church meetings are designed to carry out the objectives that the students lived under in Bible college conditions. Preaching well-prepared sermons has now become the goal rather than producing disciples to do the work of the ministry. Our rich, undiluted love for Scripture and communicating truth has caused some churches to neglect other significant aspects of life in the Kingdom. Body ministry is a fundamental biblical principle that is largely ignored in many places. If all we are is pew food for the teaching and preaching of a small number of "qualified" people, we are never going to grow up into all things in God.

The questions that leaders must ask are. What? - and Why? What are we doing, and why are we doing it? Does our church structure, culture, and model-give somebody the use of itself to drawing people into a deeper experience of God, the practice of truth, and into pathways of service and supernatural expression?

A key question concerns the development of worship and love for God. "Are we giving enough place to the scriptural and practical outworking involved in creating new expressions of adoration, devotion, and worship?" Worship must grow through ongoing development of devotion.

Do we actually train people how to worship in song, dance, and creative expression? Do we have devotional courses that develop people in their personal quiet times with God? Does our church know the difference between personal worship where we all sing together, and corporate worship where we deliberately enter into a communal and focused activity in order to minister to God?

We are not good at balancing truth with experience and practice. We have emphasized correct doctrine and an understanding of Scripture but have neglected the importance of experience in the development of mature believers. Biblical orthodox has become a barren wilderness of organized religion. We defend the truth to the death, which is very admirable, but we do not live it out to the full. Our greatest strength has become our most telling weakness. Without experience our relationship with God has nowhere to go. It is like knowing everything about romantic loving relationships but never getting married. All your knowledge is merely study notes in a book. The experience of the relationship enables us to write the truth on the tables of our heart, which is a poetic way of referring to experience.

I am always intrigued by what God does not say as well as by what He conveys in our lives. As humans we like structure, organization, form, and substance. We want detailed information because we like to know what God is doing and where He is taking us. Abraham, though, had to go out not knowing where He was going.

Hebrews 11:8 By faith Abraham, when he was called to go out into a place which he should after receive for an inheritance, obeyed; and he went out, not knowing whither he went.

Sometimes God does not give us detailed vision because He wants us to walk by faith. He will give us broad parameters rather than specific objectives. Vision is something we see in part and know in part, just like prophecy. God gives us enough to broadly see the next step or couple of stages but no more. When we fulfill those goals, we receive more insight and direction.

God is vague about meetings. He really says only two things.

Hebrews 10:25 Not forsaking the assembling of ourselves together, as the manner of some *is;* but exhorting *one another:* and so much the more, as ye see the day approaching.

1 Corinthians 14:26-33 How is it then, brethren? when ye come together, every one of you hath a psalm, hath a doctrine, hath a tongue, hath a revelation, hath an interpretation. Let all things be done unto edifying. If any man speak in an *unknown* tongue, *let it be* by two, or at the most *by* three, and

that by course; and let one interpret. But if there be no interpreter, let him keep silence in the church; and let him speak to himself, and to God. Let the prophets speak two or three, and let the other judge. If *any thing* be revealed to another that sitteth by, let the first hold his peace. For ye may all prophesy one by one, that all may learn, and all may be comforted. And the spirits of the prophets are subject to the prophets. For God is not *the author* of confusion, but of peace, as in all churches of the saints.

This passage does not give detailed information on how to run meetings. If it did, most church meetings would be unbiblical! It talks about possibilities and what may happen. Interestingly, it is all concerned with supernatural utterance, which probably does not apply to a lot of churches. Does the lack of supernatural utterance in our churches make us unbiblical? It's just a question. This passage does not speak of form or structure. There is no detail regarding when to sing, teach, pray, or otherwise. It only speaks of creativity and degrees of spontaneity arising out of our relationship with the Holy Spirit. I am not saying that every meeting must be open, creative, and totally spontaneous.

Every meeting cannot be the same. By trying to fit people into a stereotypical meeting, we are not putting God or them first. Meetings should be designed around objectives. If our objective is to teach people how to worship God corporately, then let us act appropriately. Let us move the chairs aside (if we can!) and allow freedom of movement and expression in a workshop atmosphere. If our objective is training, let us have a seminar-type session in whatever style is appropriate for interactive learning. If our intention is to enable members to contribute openly what they feel the Holy Spirit is saying, then we need to set our stall out accordingly.

Most Sunday services are boringly familiar. In some places the order of service is made known before the meeting, rather like McDonalds. Perhaps the only real difference between some churches and McDonalds is the fact that a fast food place is cheaper, the atmosphere is better, we are in and out in no time, and we've probably been better fed! Stereotypical services produce stereotypical believers. God is endlessly creative. His nature is a challenge to any one-dimensional state. If they are for God, then let us structure them as He wills, bearing in mind His creative nature. If they are for people, then let us form the meeting to suit the objective we have in mind. If we arrange our meetings in a set formula because we have always done it that way, then we have missed the point entirely and become unbiblical in the process. If the stereotype is simply our best way to administrate people, time availability, and resources, then we need to drastically rethink what church is really all about.

God is vague about the operation of church at times, wanting us to learn sensitivity as we are led by the Spirit. The Scriptures often speak about task, operation, and purpose without specifying shape, patterns, or models. The reason for this is that the form we are working in will constantly change, whereas the task and operation may remain quite constant. The form is the wineskin that needs to be constantly oiled on the outside to retain its supple shape so that new wine will not crack it open. Similarly, the form and shape of the church need to be constantly adjusted to keep pace with the ongoing nature of the work of God.

Human beings will always set things in concrete for the sake of stability, safety, and security. That is very creditable, but it actually works against us. Our security is only in God and one another. Security comes from relationships of grace and love, not from organizational structure. If our structure is set in concrete, it will have to be overthrown if God is to continue with us in power and purpose. It is so unfortunate that the Lord has to set in motion a whole series of events just to break into our structures! People misconstrue this as warfare and resist it, which often leads to church splits. It is never the Holy Spirit who splits the church. It is usually the wineskin that has become dry and cracked and cannot handle the new thing that God wants to introduce. We try our hand at compromise, which is like patching an old garment with new cloth it will not work!

When our safety and security in the form of what we have produced is threatened, many people resist the change that God wants to bring. Even when the Bible does define a model or a pattern, the language it uses is not too descriptive. The model will be limited in terms of long-term identity. Models do not last for years; they change constantly. The changes may be subtle in order to take into account what is happening with people. Our goal is to make people change, to transform them into the image of Jesus. For that change to become complete, we must alter the model and form we build around them. As the people change, the wineskin must change. If people change but the form and structure of the church remains stagnant, we will be in serious trouble with the Holy Spirit. Leaders who do not change can only be replaced.

The apostle Paul remarked that people should follow him in as much as he was following Christ. God is vague about patterns, models, operation of church, and form and structure because He knows that the culture of different nations would make it impossible for a one-dimensional Church to exist. They would be imprisoned and murdered for their faith as they are currently in many countries. Christians are forbidden to meet publicly in many nations. Does that make them unbiblical? The Bible is vague about form and structure because the chief principle we are working to is one of being led by the Spirit.

Churches will change as people respond to the Lord and grow into levels of maturity. Cultural restrictions also play a big part in the changing nature of church. Whether that culture is caused by different national characteristics or simply by the difference between youth and elderly; street people and upper middle class society; the intelligence or the illiterate all will have a bearing on how we operate as a church.

One of the biggest problems we have in building church is changing the stereotype that certain companies of people have produced. If we are wedded more to our structure than we are to the Lord, then we have made an idol of what we have produced. It will have to come down, for God will be against it. Anything that prevents God from moving amongst His people will be overthrown by the Holy Spirit. This happens when God demonstrates through willing people all that He wants to do and be to His bride. Sadly, these people are labeled disruptive, un-teachable, and rebellious. To be fair, some of them may not have been able to contain their frustration, but that does not make them rebels.

The fivefold ministries of apostle, prophet, pastor, teacher, and evangelist will understand the pressures of growth, creativity, the development of maturity, and the production of anointed people who can fight. Each in their own way will contribute to the building of the prototype of a new church that needs to live on the battlefield. Each of them has a cutting edge that is designed to be attacking, stimulating, and provocative. Apostles are against mediocrity in any form. They will attack false ministries, false motives, and false lifestyles.

Paul continually campaigned for moral purity, relational harmony, and doctrinal clarity. He attacked and opposed people who defied God in those areas. Prophets attack injustice, unethical behavior, oppressive regimes, and stereotypical barriers to what the Lord wants to do. They are a stimulus to holiness of life and loving relationships. I get flack when I walk in my Office of an Apostle. Apostles provoke the Church to hear the now word of God and make all necessary adjustments. Teachers are given to stimulate the marriage of truth with discipleship and knowledge with experience. They attack ignorance and unbelief. They know that whenever the real truth is taught, it will cause a crisis. Anyone who is not living a life compatible with Scripture will come into conflict with the Holy Spirit.

Teachers know that Spirit-induced crisis must lead to the process and development of mature response through repentance and obedience. That is why all truth must be followed up. If it is not, then condemnation will result because the enemy will fill the vacuum if no repentant response occurs.

Pastors will be a part of this process of change, working with teachers to produce a positive belief system that can terminally change our behavior. Pastors practice the art of loving confrontation as they deal with tensions, conflicts, acts of rebellion, and people's historical baggage.

Evangelists have to stand against worldly value systems and fake philosophies as they engage a sin-sick world with the gospel. The message of the gospel is contentious, controversial, and confrontational one permeated with the revelation of the goodness, kindness, and mercy of a loving God who paid the price for us to enter His presence for all eternity.

I hope that we may understand process and the crisis that often precedes it. The conclusions we come to about our own work will be critical to our development and future.

Chapter Seventeen
Creative Thoughts

Within every believer there is within them the ability to experience creative thoughts. This will change your life if you receive what I'm saying in this Chapter. Here is a deeper understanding on the mind, specifically the creative power of thoughts.

Romans 12:2 And be not conformed to this world: but be ye transformed by the renewing of your mind, that ye may prove what *is* that good, and acceptable, and perfect, will of God.

Our entire lives will be transformed and metamorphosed when our minds are renewed. This will allow us to soar and not have to conform to the world's standards of living and being; we'll be fully capable of proving the good and acceptable and perfect will of God.

A mindset is when our minds are programmed and set to respond a specific way or project a certain impression when encountering different words, pictures, situations, etc. They have preconceived thoughts and feelings about church because of previous experiences that have been grafted into their minds: a church they attended when they were younger, a religious fanatic they watched on television, or the enthusiastic preacher on the car radio.

That mindset, is about to be changed and renewed. The Bride of Christ is about to become a very heavenly creature. Ungodly and worldly mindsets are spiritual strongholds that restrain us from soaring. These bondages are broken by the transformation that comes from the pressure and isolation in the cocoon.

We are liberated through the constrictions and pressures that the Lord allows to come upon us in the cocoon. The restraints of self-dependence are broken as we rely more and more on the Spirit of God, being strengthened in our inner person so we can rise to higher altitudes. Those who want to avoid these trials will be confined as worms to the earth. We can choose to move with the current of the Spirit and let the trials of this present age work for us, or we can continue to wade through the shallow water and never reach our destination, which only comes after the rapids. Jesus said,

Matthew 10:39 He that findeth his life shall lose it: and he that loseth his life for my sake shall find it.

Paul said the sufferings and tribulations of this present age are not even worthy to be compared to the Glory that will be revealed to us, in us, and through us.

Romans 8:18 For I reckon that the sufferings of this present time *are* not worthy *to be compared* with the glory which shall be revealed in us.

Unfortunately, many leaders, from a lack of maturity, have restrained and kept the Church in a state of infancy; they are in danger of loosing all. This metamorphosis is mandatory. Trying to save someone from it is doing him harm. The chick needs the struggle of getting out of the egg to produce blood flow into its extremities. If not, there's a good chance of loosing its life after birth. The struggle for life is necessary for walking in the fullness of life.

Humans and God, have a creative ability that can be exercised through the mind to recreate the world around us

Psalms 139:14 I will praise thee; for I am fearfully *and* wonderfully made: marvellous *are* thy works; and *that* my soul knoweth right well.

We were created in the image and likeness of God The same creative nature of God is resident within humankind. Creative authority is best released through love the most excellent way. With all that has been given to humanity in terms of the gifts of the Holy Spirit and the ability to cooperate with the Spirit of God in the anointing, there still remains a fuller and more abundant way to minister the mind, heart, and power of God in the earth.

1 Corinthians 12:31 But covet earnestly the best gifts: and yet shew I unto you a more excellent way.

1 Corinthians 13:9-13 For we know in part, and we prophesy in part. But when that which is perfect is come, then that which is in part shall be done away. When I was a child, I spake as a child, I understood as a child, I thought as a child: but when I became a man, I put away childish things. For now we see through a glass, darkly; but then face to face: now I know in part; but then shall I know even as also I am known. And now abideth faith, hope, charity, these three; but the greatest of these *is* charity.

Many people take the phrase, "when the perfect comes," and conclude it is referring to the second coming of Christ. The phrase, however, is talking about love. The whole chapter is talking about love and our lives being perfected in love. Paul is talking about a new standard, a new level. He says we should earnestly desire the best gifts and graces, but there still is a better way the way of love.

Galatians 5:6 For in Jesus Christ neither circumcision availeth any thing, nor uncircumcision; but faith which worketh by love.

When that which is perfect is come, looking through a glass darkly will be done away with. We will come to this perfection of love from one level to another more fully, deeply, and intimately.

It is important for us to keep in mind that thoughts are seeds Thoughts have life in them and will reproduce, this simply means all things reproduce after their own kind.

Galatians 1:11, 12 But I certify you, brethren, that the gospel which was preached of me is not after man. For I neither received it of man, neither was I taught *it*, but by the revelation of Jesus Christ.

This creation law affects us continually as it shapes our future and determines our present. Even now our circumstances are being determined by this law. We need to stop blaming everybody and their brother, including the devil, for our present circumstances and to take responsibility for what is growing in our lives. This creation law is irrevocable and unchangeable. We plant trees and gardens, and they reproduce after their kind. The fertile soil where we unknowingly plant most seeds is in the garden of our heart. What you plant there will reproduce and come forth. Thoughts are simply seeds. Passion and strong desire are the heat that causes the seed to spin into life. Babies are conceived in passion. So too, inner passion gives life to the seeds in our heart.

Proverbs 23:7 For as he thinketh in his heart, so *is* he: Eat and drink, saith he to thee; but his heart *is* not with thee.

This means that as a person believes and thinks in his heart, so he will become. What he thinks about will be manifested in his life.

Matthew 7:1, 2 Judge not, that ye be not judged. For with what judgment ye judge, ye shall be judged: and with what measure ye mete, it shall be measured to you again.

The seed of judgment sown will reap a tree of judgment. Because of this law, we must live every moment, in thought and action, as we desire the future to be. The human mind is one of the greatest earthly powers.

Mark 11:23 For verily I say unto you, That whosoever shall say unto this mountain, Be thou removed, and be thou cast into the sea; and shall not doubt in his heart, but shall believe that those things which he saith shall come to pass; he shall have whatsoever he saith.

Jesus isn't speaking metaphorically He's talking literally. You don't even have to be a Christian for this to work. There are many people displaying supernatural feats and abilities illegally by this principle alone. Remember, the human mind is a great earthly power; this universal law cannot be changed.

Mark 11:24 Therefore I say unto you, What things soever ye desire, when ye pray, believe that ye receive *them*, and ye shall have *them*.

Jesus is saying to believe, be confident, and desire what you are asking for and you will receive it. Our thoughts aren't momentary insignificant wisps but are the seeds of desire that produce and chart the course of our present and future life. If thoughts are seeds, then how are they planted? When a thought firmly connects with emotion, a supernatural power or force is released. If you hold your thoughts until they are connected with your emotions, feelings, and desires, it releases the power of life and light. This principle is similar to

Matthew 18:19 Again I say unto you, That if two of you shall agree on earth as touching any thing that they shall ask, it shall be done for them of my Father which is in heaven.

When your emotions agree with your thinking, it shall be done! This is the power of union and agreement. It works for both God-thoughts and demonic thoughts. This seed of thought, when energized by emotion, will literally create an environment of love and joy around your entire household. Any thoughts that connect with our emotions become a very strong power and determine the atmosphere around us.

The Church has taught for years that emotions are not important. I say to you that emotions as well as your thought life are the creative side of you. Your emotions are essential for everything to happen. Jesus was moved with an emotion called compassion and released miracles.

Matthew 20:34 So Jesus had compassion *on them,* and touched their eyes: and immediately their eyes received sight, and they followed him.

Mark 1:41 And Jesus, moved with compassion, put forth *his* hand, and touched him, and saith unto him, I will; be thou clean.

Compassion releases miracles, even the raising of the dead.

Luke 7:11-17 And it came to pass the day after, that he went into a city called Nain; and many of his disciples went with him, and much people. Now when he came nigh to the gate of the city, behold, there was a dead man carried out, the only son of his mother, and she was a widow: and much people of the city was with her. And when the Lord saw her, he had compassion on her, and said unto her, Weep not. And he came and touched the bier: and they that bare *him* stood still. And he said, Young man, I say unto thee, Arise. And he that was dead sat up, and began to speak. And he delivered him to his mother. And there came a fear on all: and they glorified God, saying, That a great prophet is risen up among us; and, That God hath visited his people. And this rumour of him went forth throughout all Judaea, and throughout all the region round about.

The power and Glory of God in the anointing are released through the gateway of human affection.

2 Corinthians 6:12 Ye are not straitened in us, but ye are straitened in your own bowels.

We have to feel what we do. When our thinking connects with our feelings, a seed is planted by desire and a power is released.

James 1:15 Then when lust hath conceived, it bringeth forth sin: and sin, when it is finished, bringeth forth death.

We need to be careful what we are thinking! Every time we think, we place a spiritual offering at the door that energizes and powers that thought. An evil desire is conceived when the thought and the emotion come together. This forms a creative power bond of agreement that brings forth death. Brings forth means to breed or create and is the same as a plant that is produced from the seed. When I meditate on the Word and revelation begins to flow, my whole being seems to be flooded with light not only light, but flooded with the tranquil peace and life of God. The revelation that is coming from God's mind flows through my emotions and makes a place in my spirit man for seed to be planted and to grow. Revelation isn't just an abstract thought; it is connected with a feeling that buries life deep inside us. Seeds are planted; conception has taken place. If watered, the revelation with give birth in our life. As a man thinks, so he will become.

This new Glory generation will move in the understanding of how to release wonders in the creative power of the imagination. They will birth the will and purposes of God in the earth with mind-blowing authority over physical elements in the natural realm. The creative power of the imagination is not a New Age or occult principle; it is a Kingdom reality created by God to manifest in the natural what is seen in the spirit. The demonic world of the occult can use it to birth destruction in the natural by curses that materialize from unholy allegiances. But God really gave us an imagination to come under the influence of the Holy Spirit and birth life, freedom, and destiny into our lives. Unfortunately, we've been taught to believe that anything to do with using our imagination is New Age and is used to advance the kingdom of darkness. In reality, New Agers and the occult stole something very precious from the saints of God and have perverted it to the point that we are afraid to come near it. It is time we take the power to envision back. It is time we start using what God has given to us to wreak havoc on the kingdom of darkness!

We must visualize what we desire to become in God. Actually, we must see ourselves as we really are in Christ; then it will manifest as reality in our lives. The imagination is a creative tool that brings into the physical world that which sits dormant in the unseen realm. We can use our imagination to transform the world around us, both for good and for evil. You cannot walk in something until you see yourself walking in it. You say, "Visualizing is New Age." You've been visualizing since you were born. Every time you think about something, every time you daydream, you're visualizing. It's part of the thinking process.

There have been a number of people throughout history who have broken through simple spiritual concepts into the upper Kingdom realities. They understood genuine Kingdom laws and began to practice them. Only a handful of people have risen to a level in God where they could overcome any earthly obstacle in life even overcoming death. Not just Enoch either. It is easy to blame the devil and others for things that happen to us in life, but in actuality our present circumstances are the direct result of where our heart is set in thought.

Matthew 5:28 But I say unto you, That whosoever looketh on a woman to lust after her hath committed adultery with her already in his heart.

Everyone who looks with his eyes and thinks in his mind has committed and birthed the act of adultery in his heart it's already done. The mind and the imagination are the same thing. It's just as if you had already done it.

In every atom there is life and light. When God created the universe, He breathed them out of His imagination. The newly created atoms were all spinning harmoniously according to their own vibration, their own unique created order However, when Adam fell from the Glory of God, the result was so dramatic that it shifted the world on its axis. The earth wasn't the only thing that shifted; each individual atom was knocked off rhythm from its original spin. Everything was affected; even at a subatomic level. When this happened, the door was wide open for satan to corrupt and alter things genetically. The good news is that all of creation was preprogrammed to respond to love. If we have love emanating out from us, the smallest atom can feel it and will respond to it. Atoms were birthed from love, and as created particles feel love and respond to it. Animals feel it, trees feel it, and all of nature feels it. Atoms will cooperate with what you desire and speak because they recognize your sonship and know that you have dominion over the world. What you emanate leaves a trail and affects everything around you. If you come home with a bad attitude, before you even open your mouth, the first thing that's going to recognize it is your cat or dog. Creation knows because it is sensitized to emotion. All of creation waits eagerly for the children of God to step into their full understanding of sonship.

Creation knows that we have the power and authority to free it from the bondage of decay, corruption, sin, and death that entered the world during the Fall.

Romans 8:19-21 For the earnest expectation of the creature waiteth for the manifestation of the sons of God. For the creature was made subject to vanity, not willingly, but by reason of him who hath subjected *the same* in hope, Because the creature itself also shall be delivered from the bondage of corruption into the glorious liberty of the children of God.

1 Corinthians 13:10 But when that which is perfect is come, then that which is in part shall be done away.

All creation responds to the more excellent and perfect way of love. It is through love that the curse will be lifted and creation will enter into freedom. Signs, wonders, and miracles come through love we just have to keep unbelief out.

Mark 9:23 Jesus said unto him, If thou canst believe, all things *are* possible to him that believeth.

I think it would be safe to say that not much is possible, then, if you don't believe James says that when we ask God for something we should do it with faith and not doubt in our hearts.

James 1:6 But let him ask in faith, nothing wavering. For he that wavereth is like a wave of the sea driven with the wind and tossed.

He continues to explain what we should expect to receive from the Lord if we do indeed harbor doubt in our hearts.

James 1:7, 8 For let not that man think that he shall receive any thing of the Lord. A double minded man *is* unstable in all his ways.

Doubt opens the door to unbelief, and unbelief is a tremendous evil power that cuts us off from the promises of God. Unbelief is a spirit that is like a dark, demonic hood of blindness and deception. We must deal violently with this spirit. We shouldn't have even a speck of doubt in our hearts. Jesus said,

Mark 1:15 And saying, The time is fulfilled, and the kingdom of God is at hand: repent ye, and believe the gospel.

Do you see that? We overcome doubt and unbelief by repenting and turning to the Lord changing our way of thinking then believing. Sometimes this takes a fierce step of faith in the right direction and a forceful decision to believe. It is necessary to learn to hold our focus on the Lord to set our thoughts and our imagination in faith until they connect with our feelings and emotions. When we continually do this, heavenly seeds are planted and faith begins to grow and flourish and come alive. We must begin to see ourselves walking in the light of these things. Start to imagine yourself walking in your future and destiny, and align yourself with the Kingdom of God. It will come to pass. This is the way it is. God did it this way in the beginning: He thought it, saw it, and spoke it—then it came into existence. Remember:

Proverbs 23:7 For as he thinketh in his heart, so *is* he: Eat and drink, saith he to thee; but his heart *is* not with thee.

We can either believe and receive or doubt and go without.

There are many things that fascinate me in God, but none have come so close to the mystery of our identity in Christ. Just thinking that we have been cut out of the same swatch of clothing as God causes me to rush with anticipation. When I think about being alive in eternity before I was born or before the worlds were created, it makes me want to know the reality of that life in eternity. I want to know what it's like and what's happening there. The reality is you are a spirit. Your spirit came from Heaven and has been in existence for a long time. Your spirit has memories of life in Heaven.

When your spirit came into your body at birth, it became wrapped in the soul and those memories began to fade and were eventually lost. Before Jesus was born on earth, He was a Spirit. He existed in the bosom of the Father. He came to earth as a Spirit and lived in a body with a soul.

John 1:18 No man hath seen God at any time; the only begotten Son, which is in the bosom of the Father, he hath declared *him*.

Now Jesus is still a Man: Spirit, soul, and body. Except He now has a resurrected body since He rose from the dead. Yes we are spirit, but God gave us a soul and body also. We are new creations in Christ.

2 Corinthians 5:17 Therefore if any man *be* in Christ, *he is* a new creature: old things are passed away; behold, all things are become new.

Yes, we are spirit beings, but we are human beings too. All of our spirit, soul, and body need to come into alignment with the Kingdom of God this only happens through the spirit first though.

1 Thessalonians 5:23 And the very God of peace sanctify you wholly; and *I pray God* your whole spirit and soul and body be preserved blameless unto the coming of our Lord Jesus Christ.

It is important that we as spirit, soul, and body blend as one so we can interact with the spiritual realm and the physical realm. Heaven was first a spiritual world. But then God created the earth and brought Heaven into it in the Garden of Eden. He brought Heaven into a physical dimension. When you were born again, Christ came into your spirit, and in that seed is the fullness of the Godhead: Father, Son, and Holy Spirit. You are filled with eternity past, present, and future.

1 John 2:20 But ye have an unction from the Holy One, and ye know all things.

Everything past, present, and future has already been written on the fabric of your spirit person. If you come into union with the Holy Spirit, you have access to know all things.

Many times while ministering, I will begin to see things through the impression of my mind in the spirit. I've learned that, when ministering in the Holy Spirit, I'm under the influence of the supernatural and that what's flowing into my mind is from Heaven. I've also learned that as I begin to speak in the natural about what I'm seeing in the spirit, it creates the framework for those things to be created in the natural. The reality of the spirit realm is all around us. Sometimes the Holy Spirit will just give you a hunch or a slight impression. But if you follow Him, you'll be surprised at what happens. Some of the most extraordinary miracles in your life will happen because you followed the tiniest nudge from the Holy Spirit.

When Abraham was an old man, God promised that his descendants would be like the stars. How was it possible for Abraham to become the father of two great nations? God told him to look into Heaven to look at the stars Abraham set his eyes to the heavens and looked He imagined He believed. This impossible situation became possible when he visualized it as a reality. As he looked at the stars, he saw his family. God wants us to be active in our part of stepping into our destinies. God speaks the promise, but we fail to look up; we fail to visualize; we fail to see the impossible situation with eyes of faith. When we use our imaginations according to the promises of God, the impossible becomes possible. God calls those things that are not as though they already exist. When the earth was formless and void, God already saw it with form and substance and simply called it forth.

2 Corinthians 4:13 We having the same spirit of faith, according as it is written, I believed, and therefore have I spoken; we also believe, and therefore speak;

If we see ourselves sick, broken down, and impoverished, that is exactly what will be birthed in our lives. If we begin to imagine ourselves as blessed of God and start calling those things that are not as though they are, they will manifest in our lives. Regardless of our race, gender, financial condition, or family situation we must believe and speak. Let's be like Abraham and look up at the stars.

Matthew 8:5-13 And when Jesus was entered into Capernaum, there came unto him a centurion, beseeching him, And saying, Lord, my servant lieth at home sick of the palsy, grievously tormented. And Jesus saith unto him, I will come and heal him. The centurion answered and said, Lord, I am not worthy that thou shouldest come under my roof: but speak the word only, and my servant shall be healed. For I am a man under authority, having soldiers under me: and I say to this *man,* Go, and he goeth; and to another, Come, and he cometh; and to my servant, Do this, and he doeth *it.* When Jesus heard *it,* he marvelled, and said to them that followed, Verily I say unto you, I have not found so great faith, no, not in Israel. And I say unto you, That many shall come from the east and west, and shall sit down with Abraham, and Isaac, and Jacob, in the kingdom of heaven. But the children of the kingdom shall be cast out into outer darkness: there shall be weeping and gnashing of teeth. And Jesus said unto the centurion, Go thy way; and as thou hast believed, *so* be it done unto thee. And his servant was healed in the selfsame hour.

I believe our imaginations are part of the creative nature of humanity. Everything God spoke into existence already existed in His mind and in His heart. Everything that a person builds first lives within him within the imagination. We know that faith is not just a matter of the mind but of the heart. When God asks us to have faith in Him, He is asking us to trust Him. Trust is a matter of the heart. But true faith doesn't just stay in the heart; indeed, faith first springs from the heart, but it eventually floods the rest of the individual including the mind, imagination, and, in time, every action and word.

In the story of the faith of the centurion, we see Jesus saying that He will come to the centurion's servant to heal him. Jesus was perfectly fine with going the distance, but the centurion believed within himself that his servant would be healed if only Jesus spoke the word. The centurion's faith rested in the spoken word. Because he was a man of authority, a man of the spoken word, he had his mind made up and was firmly convinced in the authority of the spoken word. It is in the way you believe, the way you imagine, and where your faith rests.

Because imagination helps cultivate faith and belief, you could say, "As you imagine, it will be done unto you." Another example of this in Scripture is the story of the woman with an issue of blood.

Mark 5:27, 28 When she had heard of Jesus, came in the press behind, and touched his garment. For she said, If I may touch but his clothes, I shall be whole.

Colossians 3:1, 2 If ye then be risen with Christ, seek those things which are above, where Christ sitteth on the right hand of God. Set your affection on things above, not on things on the earth.

As we fix our eyes on Jesus and keep seeking the things above with our minds and imaginations, we will get breakthrough we will literally get to see the eternal realm. When we glimpse Jesus, everything will be changed. In this process, we must use our imaginations to reconstruct our entire thought lives. We must learn to take every thought captive to the obedience of Christ and set our affections on things above.

2 Corinthians 10:5 Casting down imaginations, and every high thing that exalteth itself against the knowledge of God, and bringing into captivity every thought to the obedience of Christ;

We will start to see ourselves and everyone around us through the eyes of Christ. We will start to *see* our destiny and our future Glory. Then, and only then, will we be able to pull it into today.

Ephesians 1:17, 18 That the God of our Lord Jesus Christ, the Father of glory, may give unto you the spirit of wisdom and revelation in the knowledge of him: The eyes of your understanding being enlightened; that ye may know what is the hope of his calling, and what the riches of the glory of his inheritance in the saints,

When we look with the eyes of understanding, we are gazing into the eternal realm the real realm. God can speak to us through the imagination, the devil can speak to us through the imagination, and we can use our own imagination. If we are imagining something from our own mind, it is coming from us. But imaginations that come from outside ourselves are coming from one of two sources: God or the devil. We can be imagining something from ourselves and then, all of a sudden, we receive something not from ourselves something from God or the devil. Where did that come from? You might think, I wasn't even thinking about that! Because you were exercising your imagination, you were open to the spirit realm. The spirit realm loves to imprint pictures and thoughts into our imaginations because our imaginations are the gateway and the link that brings the spiritual into the natural. If someone constantly receives ungodly images, they may just think it's their own imagination. In reality they actually have a demonic spirit lodged in their mind. That demonic spirit is the gatekeeper to the imagination; he guards what comes in and what goes out. Our spirit, as one with the Holy Spirit, should be the gatekeeper to our imaginations. This is why it's vital that our minds are washed with pure water so those strongholds in the mind and imagination can be broken and replaced.

When we find our mind wandering randomly and it leads us into perverseness, it's an indicator that there are strongholds in the mind and that we need deliverance. Deliverance is as simple as starving those strongholds and thoughts and having the powerful blood of Jesus Christ wash over us. We are the keepers of our minds; we must guard what comes into our eye-gates and ear-gates. When daydreaming, either you started it or someone else did. The spirit world always wants to communicate with us. The vast majority of God's communication with people in the Scriptures came in visions and dreams. Remember, as a person thinks in his heart, so he becomes. Someone else has access to our minds other than us. Who is it? Learn to see for yourself. Accept the good and reject the evil. Train your mind and exercise your spiritual senses to discern the voice of God from among all the other voices. If you want to walk with God, you will have to learn to walk with Him in your imagination, having the eyes of your understanding enlightened that you may know the things of God.

The imagination is our gift from God that should be used as a tool to create and manifest the unseen into the seen. God has created us to be a thinking, imaginative, and visionary people who, with the sanctified imagination, like God.

Romans 4:17 (As it is written, I have made thee a father of many nations,) before him whom he believed, *even* God, who quickeneth the dead, and calleth those things which be not as though they were.

God has given us the power to create, and not just through procreation or reproduction, but in many different ways including artistically and visually. We are inventive and creative like our Father in Heaven. Every physical item that surrounds you right now, whether it's a clock, a picture frame, or a coffee cup, has a certain amount of imagination and creative design put into it. Every masterpiece ever created first existed in the imagination of the artist.

It is important that we see ourselves the way God sees us. We are citizens of Heaven. We must be transformed from natural ways of thinking to heavenly ways. God breathed the breath of life into Adam and he became the first living soul. When God breathed the breath of life, He breathed all eternity into Adam. Adam's destiny, identity, citizenship, origin, imagination, and the Spirit of Wisdom and Understanding all came out of the eternity of eternities, directly out of God, and into Adam.

Psalms 139:13-17 For thou hast possessed my reins: thou hast covered me in my mother's womb. I will praise thee; for I am fearfully *and* wonderfully made: marvellous *are* thy works; and *that* my soul knoweth right well. My substance was not hid from thee, when I was made in secret, *and* curiously wrought in the lowest parts of the earth. Thine eyes did see my substance, yet being unperfect; and in thy book all *my members* were written, *which* in continuance were fashioned, when *as yet there was* none of them. How precious also are thy thoughts unto me, O God! how great is the sum of them!

We are citizens of Heaven; our origin is not from here. We are the very offspring of God. Doesn't this tell us something of our ability to access the very home from which we came? We can use our imaginations to creatively bring into the natural that which exists in the spirit. We can release the will of God for our families, friends, ministries, businesses, cities, states, and the nations. So what's on your heart? What is your vision?

You have a blueprint and destiny from God within your spirit that's unchangeable. Most often the desires in our hearts are the very things God has sealed and ordered in us by the Holy Spirit. We are capable of bringing out and birthing our destinies. If we don't, we will agonize over it until it happens. Many of us wonder what the will of God is for our lives when it's already written all over us

God gave me a new word in the Litchfield Revival. It's Visionating. This is when your imagination gets consumed by God's very thoughts. There are times when I'm alone with the Lord in the

Spirit and I find myself visualizing and screaming out for the things I dream about: healing the masses, casting out demons with a word, God backing up my words with powerful signs and wonders. I imagine the Glory of God sweeping over a football field-sized amphitheater with Holy Spirit power and fire wiping out the whole place. I visualize the power of God covering a whole city, everybody getting saved, and miracles and healings being demonstrated in power by His radiant Glory! Then I listen to the people come into the great congregation of the Lord and testify of what great things God has done for them, person after person coming forward to testify These things will happen in my lifetime because I can see them! I've been to many of these events in the Spirit and they are wonderful. God has put it in me to call these things forth. They will happen, and I will be a part of facilitating these mighty acts of God.

Proverbs 29:18 Where *there is* no vision, the people perish: but he that keepeth the law, happy *is* he.

I'm going as far as to say that unless we visualize and give expression to these prophetic dreams and visions that come from the Holy One living inside us, we will begin to dry up on the vine and lose hope and courage. If that happens, eventually we might settle for far less than God's most perfect will for ourselves. We've been told for too long that we can't use our imaginations to engage God. But I'm saying you can. You are free under the direction of the Holy Spirit to engage the third heavens and to uncover truths and mysteries in the Kingdom of God.

If we're hungry about moving in the same kinds of experiences Ezekiel or Isaiah had, we need to start meditating over their third Heaven experiences and start asking the Lord for our own. We need to take time to soak in the powerful presence of the Holy Spirit and use our imagination to engage Heaven based on what John saw in Revelation and what Daniel and Ezekiel and Isaiah saw. When we engage ourselves in this manner, it's only a matter of time before we are before the very throne of God ourselves.

Unless we exercise our imaginations in a sanctified manner as God intended and take back the right to use our imaginations from the devil, we will be at a great disadvantage. God loves dreamers and visionaries who believe His Word. We need to get a hold of God and let Him get a hold of us. We need to shake Heaven until we see the full fruit of our heart's desires come to pass.

Chapter Eighteen
Rise Up or Die

We must rise up or we might as well just lie down and die. This was a Word of the Lord spoken to the Waves of Revival Body of Believers. America is suffering under a vacuum of leadership. This is not just in government but also in virtually every major center of influence, including the church. In Isaiah chapters three through five, we are told that capricious, immature leaders are the beginning of the judgment of God for the nation that turns from God and falls to the ultimate depravity of calling good evil and evil good, and for dishonoring the honorable while honoring the dishonorable. That is an accurate description of America. It will take more than an election to get us out of the mire we're in. We must have revival. We must have another Great Awakening or we will not survive much longer.

America needs to get ready. This is not to imply that the elections are not important. America and the rest of Western civilization have been led to the edge of a most dangerous cliff. The whole world is about to crash on the rocks of financial bankruptcy, but financial problems are just a root of something worse. The West has lost its spiritual and moral underpinnings without which we cannot survive as a free people.

Money is not the answer to America's problems. A financial change of direction could buy us more time, but without a change of heart, we will end up at the same place very quickly. America has fallen into virtually every trap that the Founding Fathers warned would doom the Nation. These warnings were specific and clear and the results of going the direction we have gone were accurately foreseen. These warnings have been repeated often from Congress and the Oval Office, but nothing has been done to change the course. Leadership requires more than knowledge of what needs to be done it requires the courage, resolve, and endurance to take the helm and steer the ship out of danger.

God is looking at the heart of America. Again, our problems are not just economic problems they are character problems. The economy is just a reflection of the sickness of heart we now have. We do need to evaluate what is being done and what the consequences will be if we do not change our course, but we also need to evaluate why we have been doing them.

We must be careful in our decisions in this hour. The whole world is entering "the valley of decision." What is going to be our decision? If we follow the crowd, we may feel more secure for a time, but we also may be putting ourselves in far more jeopardy. The same crowd that welcomed Jesus into Jerusalem by crying, "Hosanna! Blessed is He who comes in the name of the Lord," were just five days later crying, "Crucify Him!" The discernment of the crowd in such matters has seldom been good. We each must have in our own core a moral compass that we will navigate by regardless of whether others are going that way or not.

Americans have lost more of their freedoms in the last three years than possibly in the last two centuries. Recent Obama Administration orders have been described as a frontal attack on the Catholic Church, but they are much more than that. They are a very basic and bold attack on the entire church in America, as well as religious liberty in America. If the church in America continues to sleep through what is being done to it, then it will very soon wake up dead.

Where are the voices like John the Baptist who would challenge Herod? This is the time for courage and unyielding resolve. If we are afraid, we will be killed like John the Baptist. We must remember that there are worse things than dying. It will be far worse to stand on that great Judgment Day as a watchman who did not sound the alarm or as a shepherd who did not protect those entrusted to them.

Revelations 21:8 But the fearful, and unbelieving, and the abominable, and murderers, and whoremongers, and sorcerers, and idolaters, and all liars, shall have their part in the lake which burneth with fire and brimstone: which is the second death.

It will be much better to suffer now, even imprisonment or death, than to suffer then. There is no place for cowardice in the true faith. The Lord made it clear that those who sought to save their lives would lose them, but those who would lose their lives for His sake would find them.

Matthew 16:25 For whosoever will save his life shall lose it: and whosoever will lose his life for my sake shall find it.

This is our time. This is our watch. Will we show the courage that is demanded of the true servants of the King?

John the Baptist, rarely had prophetic experiences, but he was a preacher of righteousness and justice with an uncompromising resolve. His message of repentance compelled the entire nation to come out and listen to him. Repentance has to be preached to prepare the way for the Lord. It is the most important message that we can preach in this hour.

Both righteousness and wickedness are what God defines, not what political correctness says they are. Not long ago, America was a nation that possibly aligned itself with God's definition of righteousness and justice possibly more than any other nation. Because of this, we received what God promised to any nation that walked in His ways. Now we are starting to suffer the consequences that He warned would come upon the nation that departed from His ways, and this began with a vacuum of leadership.

The answer is not to pursue leadership, but to pursue the repentance that will lead us back to God's favor, and then He will raise up righteous leaders.

2 Chronicles 7:14 If my people, which are called by my name, shall humble themselves, and pray, and seek my face, and turn from their wicked ways; then will I hear from heaven, and will forgive their sin, and will heal their land.

Here we see that the Lord requires four things to heal a land:
- Humility
- Prayer
- Seeking His face
- Repentance from wickedness

These are required of the Lord's people, not the heathen. It seems that a new humility is coming upon much of the church, which is encouraging. We also have had some of the greatest prayer movements in history raised up in recent times. Multitudes of Christians, especially youth, are now seeking an intimate relationship with the Lord. These are all very encouraging signs. However, there has been little or no repentance from wickedness. In-depth studies reveal that even the most devout Christian groups have fallen to such a level of unrighteousness and the sins that the Lord called "wickedness" that Christians are no longer distinguishable from non-Christians in basic morality and integrity. This is an appalling and biblically terrifying state for the church in America. It has happened on our watch.

Eli had been a faithful priest in the house of the Lord his whole life. He loved the Lord so much that when he received the news that the ark of God had been captured by the Philistines, he fell over and died. Yet he was given one of the worst rebukes from the Lord in Scripture. Why?

The first word from the Lord that Samuel received was condemnation for Eli because he had let his sons fall into wickedness and bring a curse upon themselves, and Eli had not rebuked them. In this message, Eli was told that sacrifices and offerings forever could not atone for this sin. Eli admitted that this was the word of the Lord, but still made no changes. Eli was not told that his sins could not be forgiven, but that all of his good works, even if done forever, could not atone for his irresponsibility of not bringing the necessary correction to those who had been entrusted to his care.

This being translated for us today would be that all of the good works and charity in the world will not atone for the failure of letting those entrusted to us fall into the iniquity and wickedness that will be their doom.

Galatians 5:19-21 Now the works of the flesh are manifest, which are *these;* Adultery, fornication, uncleanness, lasciviousness, Idolatry, witchcraft, hatred, variance, emulations, wrath, strife, seditions, heresies, Envyings, murders, drunkenness, revellings, and such like: of the which I tell you before, as I have also told *you* in time past, that they which do such things shall not inherit the kingdom of God.

If we have given our lives to Christ and we continue to live according to the flesh as described here, the message is just as clear in the other primary books of the New Testament, such as the Book of Romans, that we will perish.

In II Timothy 4, the Apostle Paul warned about the time when a great deception would come upon believers because they would "only want to have their ears tickled" or could only hear positive things. Much of the body of Christ in America has fallen to that state now since they will automatically reject anything they consider to be negative. As both the Lord and His apostles warned, such are heading for a terrible end.

An abundance of teachers and teachings today can make people feel better about themselves, even though their eternal lives are in jeopardy. Such teachings have so watered down the clear teachings of Scripture that they can make people feel comfortable in your sin, but they are deceiving you. Even the most devout can stumble at times; however, they will not rationalize their sin but rather repent. To repent means to both feel remorse and to turn from the sin.

Doctrines are now being promoted that since the New Covenant was established, the Lord no longer judges.

1 Peter 4:17 For the time *is come* that judgment must begin at the house of God: and if *it* first *begin* at us, what shall the end *be* of them that obey not the gospel of God?

The New Testament is also clear about the judgment that will come upon those who so dilute His Word as to become stumbling blocks to His people.

I have been stretched far beyond my own reasoning as I have beheld the mercy and grace of God for sinners. That He would love us so much to go to the cross as He did will be a marvel for all of eternity. That we can behold His patience in our own times because He does not want any to perish is a marvel. Even so, as the New Testament also makes clear, there is a limit to His patience, and we are foolish to presume upon it.

Romans 11:22 Behold therefore the goodness and severity of God: on them which fell, severity; but toward thee, goodness, if thou continue in *his* goodness: otherwise thou also shalt be cut off.

Those who can only see His kindness without seeing His severity do not see Him as He is. Those who only see His severity without seeing His kindness do not see Him as He is. He is both kind and severe, and those who see Him as He is see both.

Judgment like the Church of America is seeing has been a long time coming. God is a righteous and just God, and all of His judgments are righteous and just. His judgments are not all negative, but can be positive, affirming the good. They can declare innocence as well as guilt. The biblical teachings on judgment have often been distorted, but the righteous always rejoice at His judgments.

Isaiah 55:12 For ye shall go out with joy, and be led forth with peace: the mountains and the hills shall break forth before you into singing, and all the trees of the field shall clap *their* hands.

The Scriptures are also clear that everyone will stand before the Judgment Seat of Christ. This will be a good thing for the righteous and only bad for the wicked.

Many types of judgment from God are in Scripture, and only one is condemnation and only one is destruction. The rest are discipline from the Lord for those whom He loves. As we read in Hebrews 12, the most frightening thing of all should be if we are still living in sin and getting away with it. This means that we are not His. If we are His sons, He will discipline us.

America has been receiving His judgments because He still loves America, and this is evidence that He has not given up on her. Like an alarm that gets continually louder if we do not wake up, His judgments are getting increasingly severe. Even insurance companies have more discernment than some Christian leaders. What these leaders have called "acts of nature," they call "acts of God," and they are.

Many of the things being released upon the world are not directly God's doing but are the removing of His restraints so that the world begins to reap what it has sown. This is clear in such places as Revelation 7. Even so, His releasing of these things is His judgment, and if we do not recognize it as such, no one will repent to keep even worse things from coming.

If this offends you, then you have a distorted, warped view of Scripture. Such will take what are in fact acts of love and interpret them as acts of condemnation. These are the ones Peter referred to as the untaught and unstable who will distort the Scriptures to their own destruction. The destruction is only necessary if we do not recognize the judgments and repent. God would much rather show mercy, but there is a time when judgment is necessary, and if this does not work, destruction follows. This is why the Lord Jesus weeps over Jerusalem. He would much rather have gathered her under His wings, but she rejected the time of her visitation, and destruction followed.

Let us repent while the judgment is still discipline, before it gets to the point of destruction. We are also told that we can judge ourselves and He will not have to do it.

1 Corinthians 11:31 For if we would judge ourselves, we should not be judged.

As the Lord Jesus made clear, if we do not humble ourselves and fall on the Rock to be broken, then the Rock will fall on us and grind us into powder. Let's take the easy way out!

America is in jeopardy. We will not survive much longer going in the direction we are headed. I know it may look like things are getting better, but when men are saying, peace and safety, that is when sudden destruction will come. We cannot look at external conditions to see how we're doing we need to look at our own hearts. If we will turn from that which will keep us from inheriting the kingdom of God, turn from our wicked ways, embracing the humility that would also compel us to pray and seek His face, it too will be evident as the rest of Galatians 5 declares:

Galatians 5:22-25 But the fruit of the Spirit is love, joy, peace, longsuffering, gentleness, goodness, faith, Meekness, temperance: against such there is no law. And they that are Christ's have crucified the flesh with the affections and lusts. If we live in the Spirit, let us also walk in the Spirit.

If we, God's people, will walk by the Spirit instead of the flesh, then He will heal our land, and He will use us to do it.

I want to note something here. We must understand this in our Land of the Free. The Obama administration finalized a radical new rule that uses the health care law to require all health insurance providers to cover abortion-inducing drugs and sterilization as well as contraception, all free of charge. The administration based the rule's religious exemption on a provision drafted by the ACLU, applying the rule even to religious organizations such as Catholic schools, hospitals, universities, and charities that oppose such things as a matter of religious belief.

WE BETTER RISE UP NOW IN PRAYER AND UNITY!!!

Chapter Nineteen
Rediscovering the Early Pathways

There are many open pathways that we can all have full access to.

Jeremiah 6:16 Thus saith the LORD, Stand ye in the ways, and see, and ask for the old paths, where *is* the good way, and walk therein, and ye shall find rest for your souls. But they said, We will not walk *therein*.

Jeremiah 18:15 Because my people hath forgotten me, they have burned incense to vanity, and they have caused them to stumble in their ways *from* the ancient paths, to walk in paths, *in* a way not cast up;

Ezekiel 36:2 Thus saith the Lord GOD; Because the enemy hath said against you, Aha, even the ancient high places are ours in possession:

Acts 3:21 Whom the heaven must receive until the times of restitution of all things, which God hath spoken by the mouth of all his holy prophets since the world began.

Jesus walked the Pathways with God and chose to follow them even unto death, opening up for us a new and living way that leads us back home to the Father. Jesus opened up the Way through the veil of His flesh He offered Himself willingly to bring us back to God He told Mary in the garden after the resurrection.

John 20:17 Jesus saith unto her, Touch me not; for I am not yet ascended to my Father: but go to my brethren, and say unto them, I ascend unto my Father, and your Father; and *to* my God, and your God.

In order to get back to Eden we need to walk the way Jesus walked His was a life of contemplation, prayer, devotion, and communion with the Father

John 14:5, 6 Thomas saith unto him, Lord, we know not whither thou goest; and how can we know the way? Jesus saith unto him, I am the way, the truth, and the life: no man cometh unto the Father, but by me.

After Adam fell from the Glory of God, the Lord God placed a cherubim with a flaming sword to keep and guard "the way" to the tree of life.

Genesis 3:22-24 And the LORD God said, Behold, the man is become as one of us, to know good and evil: and now, lest he put forth his hand, and take also of the tree of life, and eat, and live for ever: Therefore the LORD God sent him forth from the garden of Eden, to till the ground from whence he was taken. So he drove out the man; and he placed at the east of the garden of Eden Cherubims, and a flaming sword which turned every way, to keep the way of the tree of life.

The ultimate pathway is Jesus. He said I am the Way.

1 Corinthians 15:21, 22 For since by man *came* death, by man *came* also the resurrection of the dead. For as in Adam all die, even so in Christ shall all be made alive.

Adam had borne the image of God and was created from the dust of the earth. He enjoyed blissful friendship with the Lord, walking and talking daily with Him as a father would enjoy his son. Our relationship to God was cut off, but Jesus, the Heavenly Man, opened up the ancient roads once again as One who bears the image of a heavenly Man. Jesus became a Life-Giving Spirit and restored humankind back to the place from which we fell.

1 Corinthians 15:45-49 And so it is written, The first man Adam was made a living soul; the last Adam *was made* a quickening spirit. Howbeit that *was* not first which is spiritual, but that which is natural; and afterward that which is spiritual. The first man *is* of the earth, earthy: the second man *is* the Lord from heaven. As *is* the earthy, such *are* they also that are earthy: and as *is* the heavenly, such *are* they also that are heavenly. And as we have borne the image of the earthy, we shall also bear the image of the heavenly.

Enoch walked with God on the ancient pathways and was no more, for God took him.

Genesis 5:22-24 And Enoch walked with God after he begat Methuselah three hundred years, and begat sons and daughters: And all the days of Enoch were three hundred sixty and five years: And Enoch walked with God: and he *was* not; for God took him.

Enoch spent so much time on these supernatural highways that God finally kept him. Enoch walked in the Heavenlies with the Lord and knew the vast resources of that place with all its limitless dimensions in the spirit realm. He was even asked to make amends between the fallen angels and the Creator. As a forerunner, Enoch was granted permission to see things few had seen. Obviously, Adam was still alive during Enoch's time on earth, and I'm certain Enoch spent much of his time speaking with him about what it was like before the Fall. I can imagine Adam sharing with Enoch how he walked with the Lord in the Garden, moving with effortless authority. Having this knowledge to draw from, Enoch had an anchor to approach God with. With the help of the angels, God granted Enoch access into His presence. He moved on the ancient pathways originally designed for humankind. His relentless quest to know God opened the heavens that were shut off to most. God is a Rewarder to those who hotly pursue Him. He wrote down many of his revelations and encounters in the heavenly realms. It was quite clear that the early church had and quoted the book of Enoch and highly valued it. Jesus, Peter, and Jude all cited passages from it. Even though it is not considered Canon, it is like other documented chronicles detailing Enoch's travels to Heaven and his communications with the Lord.

From the beginning of time, God has always longed for a people that would be completely His as family in the earth that He could share His heart and the secrets of the universe with. Knowing the beginning from the end it was an act worthy of pursuit, knowing there would one day be a people that would not turn their back on Him or push Him away. After being delivered from Egypt through incredible signs and wonders, the children of Israel had been offered an invitation as a nation to come up on the mountain and see the Glory of God as Moses did. God was wanting all of His children to know Him and shine with His Glory as Moses did, but instead, after being prepared three days, they turned the invitation of the Lord down because they were afraid of His presence.

Exodus 19:1-20 In the third month, when the children of Israel were gone forth out of the land of Egypt, the same day came they *into* the wilderness of Sinai. For they were departed from Rephidim, and were come *to* the desert of Sinai, and had pitched in the wilderness; and there Israel camped before the mount. And Moses went up unto God, and the LORD called unto him out of the mountain, saying, Thus shalt thou say to the house of Jacob, and tell the children of Israel; Ye have seen what I did unto the Egyptians, and *how* I bare you on eagles' wings, and brought you unto myself. Now therefore, if ye will obey my voice indeed, and keep my covenant, then ye shall be a peculiar treasure unto me above all people: for all the earth *is* mine: And ye shall be unto me a kingdom of priests, and an holy nation. These *are* the words which thou shalt speak unto the children of Israel. And Moses came and called for the elders of the people, and laid before their faces all these words which the LORD commanded him. And all the people answered together, and said, All that the LORD hath spoken we will do. And Moses returned the words of the people unto the LORD. And the LORD said unto Moses, Lo, I come unto thee in a thick cloud, that the people may hear when I speak with thee, and believe thee for ever. And Moses told the words of the people unto the LORD. And the LORD said unto Moses, Go unto the people, and sanctify them to day and to morrow, and let them wash their clothes, And be ready against the third day: for the third day the LORD will come down in the sight of all the people upon mount Sinai. And thou shalt set bounds unto the people round about, saying, Take heed to yourselves, *that ye* go *not* up into the mount, or touch the border of it: whosoever toucheth the mount shall be surely put to death: There shall not an hand touch it, but he shall surely be stoned, or shot through; whether *it be* beast or man, it shall not live: when the trumpet soundeth long, they shall come up to the mount. And Moses went down from the mount unto the people, and sanctified the people; and they washed their clothes. And he said unto the people, Be ready against the third day: come not at *your* wives. And it came to pass on the third day in the morning, that there were thunders and lightnings, and a thick cloud upon the mount, and the voice of the trumpet exceeding loud; so that all the people that *was* in the camp trembled. And Moses brought forth the people out of the camp to meet with God; and they stood at the nether part of the mount. And mount Sinai was altogether on a smoke, because the LORD descended upon it in fire: and the smoke thereof ascended as the smoke of a furnace, and the whole mount quaked greatly. And when the voice of the trumpet sounded long, and waxed louder and louder, Moses spake, and God answered him by a voice. And the LORD came down upon mount Sinai, on the top of the mount: and the LORD called Moses *up* to the top of the mount; and Moses went up.

The invitation was for all of Israel to come on the mountain into the Glory of God, seeing His Glory and being transformed in His presence. But fear caused them to shy away. They refused God for fear of dying on the mountain.

Exodus 20:18-21 And all the people saw the thunderings, and the lightnings, and the noise of the trumpet, and the mountain smoking: and when the people saw *it,* they removed, and stood afar off. And they said unto Moses, Speak thou with us, and we will hear: but let not God speak with us, lest we die. And Moses said unto the people, Fear not: for God is come to prove you, and that his fear may be before your faces, that ye sin not. And the people stood afar off, and Moses drew near unto the thick darkness where God *was*.

The Lord wanted all of His people to shine with His Glory like Moses. They had seen the power of His signs and wonders and how God had crushed the strongest nation on the planet, delivering them from bondage with raw supernatural authority never witnessed before. Seeing all these things, they still refused His invitation to come up into the mountain of His presence. They were just too afraid of the power of His majesty. Not too much further down the road, Moses had sent out ten spies to search out the land God had sworn to give the Israelites as an inheritance for them. The spies were gone forty days scouting the land. When they returned they brought fruit from the Promised Land.

Numbers 13:30-33 And Caleb stilled the people before Moses, and said, Let us go up at once, and possess it; for we are well able to overcome it. But the men that went up with him said, We be not able to go up against the people; for they *are* stronger than we. And they brought up an evil report of the land which they had searched unto the children of Israel, saying, The land, through which we have gone to search it, *is* a land that eateth up the inhabitants thereof; and all the people that we saw in it *are* men of a great stature. And there we saw the giants, the sons of Anak, *which come* of the giants: and we were in our own sight as grasshoppers, and so we were in their sight.

So the people were afraid to enter the land for fear of the giants. They talked about choosing for themselves a new captain and returning to the land of Egypt.

But Moses and Aaron fell on their faces before all the assembly of the Israelites. Joshua and Caleb tried to quiet the people and talk sense to them.

Numbers 14:8, 9 If the LORD delight in us, then he will bring us into this land, and give it us; a land which floweth with milk and honey. Only rebel not ye against the LORD, neither fear ye the people of the land; for they *are* bread for us: their defence is departed from them, and the LORD *is* with us: fear them not.

The congregation wouldn't hear what Joshua and Caleb had to say. They had made up their minds. They were going to stone Joshua and Caleb with stones and make a plan to return to the land of Egypt.

Numbers 14:10-19 But all the congregation bade stone them with stones. And the glory of the LORD appeared in the tabernacle of the congregation before all the children of Israel. And the LORD said unto Moses, How long will this people provoke me? and how long will it be ere they believe me, for all the signs which I have shewed among them? I will smite them with the pestilence, and disinherit them, and will make of thee a greater nation and mightier than they. And Moses said unto the LORD, Then the Egyptians shall hear *it,* (for thou broughtest up this people in thy might from among them;) And they will tell *it* to the inhabitants of this land: *for* they have heard that thou LORD *art* among this people, that thou LORD art seen face to face, and *that* thy cloud standeth over them, and *that* thou goest before them, by day time in a pillar of a cloud, and in a pillar of fire by night. Now *if* thou shalt kill *all* this people as one man, then the nations which have heard the fame of thee will speak, saying, Because the LORD was not able to bring this people into the land which he sware unto them, therefore he hath slain them in the wilderness. And now, I beseech thee, let the power of my Lord be great, according as thou hast spoken, saying, The LORD *is* longsuffering, and of great mercy, forgiving iniquity and transgression, and by no means clearing *the guilty*, visiting the iniquity of the fathers upon the children unto the third and fourth *generation*. Pardon, I beseech thee, the iniquity of this people according unto the greatness of thy mercy, and as thou hast forgiven this people, from Egypt even until now.

The Lord was so upset with the children of Israel that He told Moses He was going to destroy them all with pestilence and disinherit them and make from Moses a nation greater and mightier than they But Moses pleaded Israel's case to God, and God listened to Moses.

Numbers 14:20, 21 And the LORD said, I have pardoned according to thy word: But *as* truly *as* I live, all the earth shall be filled with the glory of the LORD.

The Lord had enough of these people. They had seen His Glory; they had witnessed His might, power, and strength. There had never been another nation that God had claimed for His own and had fought for. These people were eyewitnesses to His majesty, and though they literally walked through the Red Sea on dry ground, being led by the supernatural cloud by day and the pillar of fire by night, they still refused to believe that God was able to drive out the giants in the land and give them rest. The Lord told Moses these people are stiff-necked. They refused to believe. God was so angry He would have killed them all as one man if it weren't for Moses. The Lord told Moses, "I have pardoned their sin according to your word, but truly as I live and as all the earth shall be filled with the glory of the Lord!" God swore by His own Name that the earth would be filled with His Glory. He would have a people that would not refuse Him, a family in the earth, that know His ways and His paths a supernatural people that know His Glory. This was the reason the Lord was angry with Israel. He revealed Himself over and over again to a stiff-necked people that chose not to believe in Him. In the history of humankind, there has never been a generation of people to be filled with the Glory of the Lord, and I believe we are this generation. We are the Glory generation! I believe we are the people God was looking for, who will reveal the knowledge of the Glory of the Lord in the earth.

Habakkuk 2:14 For the earth shall be filled with the knowledge of the glory of the LORD, as the waters cover the sea.

There is a Glory generation already shining with the radiance and splendor of His light. This body will not just have faith in God but will have the faith *of* God. They will look and act like God in the earth. They will understand that they too are filled with the fullness of the Godhead Father, Son, and Holy Spirit and the Spirit of Holiness and resurrection power lives in them. They will become the gateway of God in the earth allowing Heaven to open up on them as Kingdom representatives. With this authority, they are able to act on God's behalf, destroying the works of the devil and establishing the will of Jesus everywhere they go. They will be filled with revelation knowledge, knowing how to implement righteousness and justice on the earth as God's magistrates and judiciaries. This is the rising Glory generation God was looking for. This is His Body on the earth. Yes, it's true Jesus Christ is coming back in the clouds one day, at the last day trump, but before that day He is coming back in and through a corporate Body of Christ in the earth. Jesus paid the ultimate price to restore us to right relationship with Himself, and now. He is reaping the fruit of tears sown in the Garden of Gethsemane. For they who sow in tears will doubtless come again rejoicing, bringing in the sheaves. Jesus Christ paid a high price in blood to restore us to this place. The fruit is ripe in the ear and ready for harvest. Now is the time. Jesus has opened up the way back to Eden; He is the Tree of Life.

Chapter Twenty
The Fire Without Being Burned

God showed me something that needs to be in this book. Many go through the Fire of God. We must be able to make it through the fire without being burned or wounded. I am aware that a bit of what I will be sharing in this closing section has been touched on before in different parts of this book. One of the main purposes in God's heart when He directed me to write on this subject. God has promised in Isaiah 43:2 that when we walk through the fire we shall not be burned, nor shall the flame scorch us. The following truths give understanding how that promise can be fulfilled.

The longer God keeps us in the fire and the hotter the flames, these are the attributes of God we'll be most tempted to doubt. When God allows us to be stripped of everything, and there's absolutely nothing left for us to depend on but His character, we had better have in-depth revelation, because in the greatest heat of the fiery trial, God can purposely withdraw all other understanding. My faith may have wavered if I had not taken much time to study God's character as a way of life. I had nothing left to cling to, or hang my faith on, when in the furnace of affliction and we can be so ill, we're incapable of discerning His voice. The greatest test of all is the perplexity test. In every other trial Perplexing and discouraging circumstances have been frequent and continual.

2 Corinthians 4:8 *We are* troubled on every side, yet not distressed; *we are* perplexed, but not in despair;

Romans 11:33 O the depth of the riches both of the wisdom and knowledge of God! how unsearchable *are* his judgments, and his ways past finding out!

But my faith hasn't failed, because the revelation of God's character is stronger than anything that has been hurled at me to convince me otherwise. Also, all throughout the continued pain, weakness, sleeplessness, and perplexities, on numerous occasions God has faithfully brought me the exact message I needed to hear. The timing of these love gifts from God has been an incredible display of His tenderness and infinite understanding.

Psalms 145:17 The LORD *is* righteous in all his ways, and holy in all his works.

Isaiah 50:10, 11 Who *is* among you that feareth the LORD, that obeyeth the voice of his servant, that walketh *in* darkness, and hath no light? let him trust in the name of the LORD, and stay upon his God. Behold, all ye that kindle a fire, that compass *yourselves* about with sparks: walk in the light of your fire, and in the sparks *that* ye have kindled. This shall ye have of mine hand; ye shall lie down in sorrow.

It always pays to keep trusting God's unswerving faithfulness, infinite wisdom and knowledge, absolute justice and unfathomable love, no matter how dark and perplexing the circumstances. He hasn't abandoned His throne, is in total control, and knows your address.

Psalms 16:8, 9 I have set the LORD always before me: because *he is* at my right hand, I shall not be moved. Therefore my heart is glad, and my glory rejoiceth: my flesh also shall rest in hope.

Psalms 34:1 ***A Psalm* of David, when he changed his behaviour before Abimelech; who drove him away, and he departed.** I will bless the LORD at all times: his praise *shall* continually *be* in my mouth.

It will not only keep our focus and perspective right, but it may well keep our sanity, it did mine. It's also a powerful means of spiritual warfare.

2 Chronicles 20:22 And when they began to sing and to praise, the LORD set ambushments against the children of Ammon, Moab, and mount Seir, which were come against Judah; and they were smitten.

Psalms 149:5, 6 Let the saints be joyful in glory: let them sing aloud upon their beds. *Let* the high *praises* of God *be* in their mouth, and a twoedged sword in their hand;

Ephesians 6:10-18 Finally, my brethren, be strong in the Lord, and in the power of his might. Put on the whole armour of God, that ye may be able to stand against the wiles of the devil. For we wrestle not against flesh and blood, but against principalities, against powers, against the rulers of the darkness of this world, against spiritual wickedness in high *places*. Wherefore take unto you the whole armour of God, that ye may be able to withstand in the evil day, and having done all, to stand. Stand therefore, having your loins girt about with truth, and having on the breastplate of righteousness; And your feet shod with the preparation of the gospel of peace; Above all, taking the shield of faith, wherewith ye shall be able to quench all the fiery darts of the wicked. And take the helmet of salvation, and the sword of the Spirit, which is the word of God: Praying always with all prayer and supplication in the Spirit, and watching thereunto with all perseverance and supplication for all saints;

David took the initiative in his battle with Goliath by declaring his faith in the name of the Lord of hosts. Then David hurried and ran to meet the Philistine giant. Either the devil is harassing us, or we're harassing him. Be on the offensive daily, and resist him in Jesus' name before he can attack us.

1 Peter 5:8, 9 Be sober, be vigilant; because your adversary the devil, as a roaring lion, walketh about, seeking whom he may devour: Whom resist stedfast in the faith, knowing that the same afflictions are accomplished in your brethren that are in the world.

If we think we can, then God may well make it hotter until we know we can't. So decide now to be open to declare your weakness and call for help. Jesus did, three times in the garden of Gethsemane. He asked for prayer support from some of His closest friends when He was facing the agonies of being separated from His Father during the times of His greatest need. This included becoming sin for all sinners, while enduring the excruciating pain of crucifixion.

Philippians 1:19 For I know that this shall turn to my salvation through your prayer, and the supply of the Spirit of Jesus Christ,

Colossians 4:3, 4 Withal praying also for us, that God would open unto us a door of utterance, to speak the mystery of Christ, for which I am also in bonds: That I may make it manifest, as I ought to speak.

David said that if it hadn't been for his delighting in God's Word, he would have perished in his affliction.

You'll see Him sovereignly adjust the temperature according to His divine purpose, not because He's capricious or whimsical. He's revealing to you that He understands your circumstances. He's in control. I have witnessed this truth on numerous occasions, and when the pain has sovereignly and temporarily lifted I have always seen God's purposes in doing so. It's been truly remarkable.

Chapter Twenty One
Choosing to Be in God's Plan

Many say they want to be part of God's Plan until they find out the cost. We must choose to be part of His plan no matter the cost.

When Balak took Balaam up to the mountain and let him look down and see the Israelites in the wilderness, Balaam had a choice. Balaam could choose to either try to curse the Israelites, or he could come down from his high and lofty, place and help them.

The choice is yours. Will the Church choose to come down from the high and lofty prideful places and help the people, or will it continue to try to curse them? The choice is yours. You're the Church. What will you choose to do? What do you want your life to be remembered for? It's time we recognize that the spirit of Balaam has run rampant in the modern Church. It's time we recognize it and drive it out, but ultimately it's your choice what you will do.

People start looking for excuses to leave churches. If people are really mature, then no matter what happens, they'll press through to what God wants them to do, not what is easiest. The point was that if you choose not to be a Christian who wants to grow up in the Lord, then he was going to go ahead and give you the excuse to leave because he wanted people in his church who would choose to move forward with the Lord.

We as the Church need to stop being immature Christians and step on over into maturity. All of this gossiping and backbiting is like being stuck in a kindergarten classroom. Can you hear the echoes of children's laughter and tears as you hear, "She hit me!" We need to stop acting like 5-year-olds in the Kingdom and start acting like mature sons and daughters in the Kingdom.

Romans 8:14 For as many as are led by the Spirit of God, they are the sons of God.

Romans 8:19 For the earnest expectation of the creature waiteth for the manifestation of the sons of God.

All of creation is waiting expectantly and longing for the sons of God to be made known. That means we must step into our sonship. We must choose to grow up and stop acting like immature children in the Kingdom.

Growing up spiritually is a choice. It's not about how many years you've been saved or how many people you've led to the Lord. It's choosing to grow up with God and move forward. You choose to mature as time progresses and God puts situations before you. We must choose to be the mature sons and daughters God has called us to be. We must choose to grow up and stop whining and complaining about who said what. Though that person hurt you, does it really matter in the grand scheme of things? Stop worrying about what they did or are doing. Be concerned about yourself.

Philippians 2:12 Wherefore, my beloved, as ye have always obeyed, not as in my presence only, but now much more in my absence, work out your own salvation with fear and trembling.

You have to work out your own salvation. You're not going to work out your brother's or your sister's, but you're going to work out your own. So stop looking at everyone else and work on yourself!

I have news for you. If you are in a church for any length of time, you will find dozens of things to get offended about. You'll find dozens of things you'll want to criticize. Holding on to all of those things will just hold you back from running your race.

I have heard over and over again on the prophetic wave that "these are days of change." Change comes as we begin to choose to walk in unity! This is beyond just something I have heard for my own life; prophetic voice after prophetic voice has confirmed it throughout the Body of Christ as a whole. But wait a minute! We're wearing ankle weights things from our past that are weighing us down. How are we supposed to swim? It is time to take off the ankle weights and swim.

Why do we hold onto "weights," or things of the past, like sacred objects? I think that sometimes it is because we lie to ourselves, thinking that by holding on to the past we are maintaining some kind of control. The root of all of that is fear. If we let go we will have to totally trust God, and that can be stepping into the unknown. If you really have a revelation of who God is, you should know by now you can trust Him.

Not that I have already obtained all this, or have already been made perfect, but I press on to take hold of that for which Christ Jesus took hold of me.

Philippians 3:13, 14 Brethren, I count not myself to have apprehended: but *this* one thing *I do,* forgetting those things which are behind, and reaching forth unto those things which are before, I press toward the mark for the prize of the high calling of God in Christ Jesus.

In order to press on, you also have to let go. You have to forget what is behind. Most of the time when we hear the word forget, we think to ourselves, How am I supposed to do that? I cannot not remember what happened. My brain just will not forget that event or time. It can start a huge cycle of self-condemnation. I have often said that, while you may not forget the event, you can forget the emotions that surrounded it like a tidal wave. Holding on to worry and anxiety is not trusting God.

Philippians 4:6 Be careful for nothing; but in every thing by prayer and supplication with thanksgiving let your requests be made known unto God.

In order for us to fully begin to swim in this change and this unity that God is leading us into, we have to take off the ankle weights. We have to trust God in what He is doing. We have to make a choice to walk away from our pasts and embrace the new. I know that can get scary.

I used to use ankle weights to work out, and after a time you tend to forget that they're even there. You are so used to being weighed down that you do not remember what it is like to be free of them.

Be free from them in Jesus' name. Let God remove the worries and the cares. Let God remove the weights of both good and bad memories. Memories are not always a bad thing, but you cannot hold onto them like a life raft and think you will swim to the places you need to swim. You have to let go now and trust God that He is with you. He will never leave you nor forsake you. His thoughts over you are good, and He has awesome things for you in this season of your life. Choose to let the weights go, and I know it will be worth it. God is excited about your future. Get excited with Him.

You can't run and hide when people hurt you and offend you. That just keeps the offense stirred up. Face it when you need to, and keep choosing to let it go. The ankle weights are keeping you back!

When you want to unload and gossip, choose not to. There is a time when you need to say something, but for the most part button your lips. Stop trying to play games with people's feelings and emotions; it just isn't worth it. Running your mouth will eventually bite you in the behind if you're not careful.

You need to become a blessing to those around you. Stop continuing to look for a blessing for yourself unless you're willing to be a blessing for others. I confess that sometimes I can be a little introverted. I can have moments where I don't want to be overly social. Sometimes I have to force myself to be an outgoing person. Every time I do, though, I'm glad I did. There is a spiritual principle of seed time and harvest. It's as if you are a farmer. You plant seeds in the ground, and you water those seeds. When the seed springs forth, then the tree bursts out of the ground and eventually bears fruit. You reap what you sow. "What goes around comes around."

You can see this in your own life as well. What seeds have you planted in relationships within the Church? Have you sowed a lot of indifference? Are you wondering now why it feels like no one really cares about you? Pardon me, but maybe it's because your indifference is showing. Have you sowed trees of gossip around you?

The place where you are today is a result of the seeds you've sown in days past. If you want good things around you, then start sowing good seeds today. Start speaking good things about those around you. Start praising people when you'd really like to smack them. When you don't have anything nice to say, don't say anything at all.

I heard a eulogy once that the best thing that could be said was that they had good teeth. Wow! That is all of life's accomplishments. Good teeth.

There are times in the Church when we must correct, and in giving this teaching, I would be wrong if I didn't bring this up. The Bible actually teaches not to have anything to do with those around you and in your churches who cause strife and division.

I appeal to you, brethren, to be on your guard concerning those who create dissensions and difficulties and cause divisions, in opposition to the doctrine (the teaching) which you have been taught. Many are thinking, What about love? Well, God still loves the person, but you become a product of the company which you hang around. You can love these people, pray for them, and be a blessing to them, but the Bible is clear that you have to be on your guard when it comes to these people. That doesn't mean you treat them like junk. But it means you must be on your guard. Don't necessarily let them into your inner circle. When you're always hearing negativity, eventually it will begin to affect you. No person is an island. People need to be around those who uplift them. If you don't want to be like the friends you're around, it's time to get new friends. I'm not saying you can't love those old friends, but you always want to have friends who are continually inspiring you to go farther with God. You always want a circle of friends who will tell you the truth in love and not try to sugarcoat everything.

Sometimes in churches, tough love has to take place. When that happens, it's not that people don't love the person, but we can't let habitual sin go on in a church member's life and not do anything about it. Don't listen to a complaint against a leader that isn't backed up by two or three responsible witnesses. If anyone falls into sin, call that person on the carpet. Those who are inclined that way will know right off they can't get by with it.

1 Timothy 5:19, 20 Against an elder receive not an accusation, but before two or three witnesses. Them that sin rebuke before all, that others also may fear.

The congregation can see what's going on and have a holy fear of getting caught in this habitual sin. It is also so that the people who are habitually sinning will realize the error of their ways and eventually be restored back to the Church. Remember, God has to discipline His children He loves, just as I would discipline my child for running toward an electrical outlet with steel wool. Discipline is showing love. Sometimes discipline in the Church may mean removing people from leadership for a period of time. If they're really working through major problems, then they need to take the time to work on their lives instead of sowing into other people's lives. That toddler has other toddlers watching him and watching you to see your reaction. Sometimes, if you don't nip one in the bud about steel wool or sin you'll have a swarm of others who are going to think that doing the same thing is OK. It will bring a watering down of the fear and reverence of the Lord unless certain actions are taken.

If we're going to stop cursing our brothers and sisters in the Lord, we need to start doing unto others what we would want done to us. Jesus commanded us to do that, but somehow over the centuries this principle appears to have been lost in the Church. We're so busy trying to get some divine revelation or God encounter that we've shuffled the basic principle of the Golden Rule back to some dusty, dirty shelf, barely caring about it. Bring it off the shelf! We all love the signs and wonders. We all love the supernatural, but in order for the commanded blessing to flow, we have to be in unity.

We want to see miracles, signs, and wonders, but our compassion has become dull and lukewarm. It's time to start praying that God would wake us up from this slumber we've been living in. I believe that the Church in America today is coming into a season when we're going to have to start relying on each other and coming together like we have never before seen in modern Church history. People in this nation have settled into a stalemate, thinking that we don't need to help each other because our government will help us. We've adapted a welfare mentality in this nation we don't need to take a step to lend a helping hand, because the government will take care of everything.

I'm sorry to tell you, Church, that our government has overextended itself like never before. Our government is not the savior of the world. Jesus Christ is our Savior. We, the Church, have a responsibility to be the hands and feet of Jesus upon the earth. I believe that the people of this nation are going to be relying more and more on the churches. I believe we're entering into a season in the modern Church when we're going to see people come into the Kingdom in numbers just like of the Acts church.

If you're used to having ten people give their lives to the Lord in one service, be ready for 50 people. If you're used to having 50 people in one service, get ready for 500. A multiplication is coming to churches that are sold out to God in this world. A multiplication of souls is coming into the Kingdom, and the churches that God has established need to get ready for all of these baby Christians. Will we be ready? Will we be ready to love them unconditionally? Will we be ready to help them grow up spiritually? Or will we be so caught up in our own agendas that we'll walk right by them and ignore their pleas for help?

It's ridiculous to think of leaving a physical baby to fend for herself. If I left a baby in a house for a couple of days by herself, it would and should be a crime. People should get arrested for that. However, we think it's fine to leave all these spiritual babies alone to fend for themselves in the Church. No! These people who are new and young in the Lord need our help. They need us to come down from our high and lofty places and help them grow up spiritually. The world is crying out for spiritual mothers and fathers to take their places in these days. We need people who will stop being so caught up in their own selfishness and be willing to sow into others so that they can go further than we ever did.

Jesus believed in sowing His life into others. Jesus sowed His life into many people, mainly His 12 disciples. Those 12 disciples changed the world. They were world-changers. Those 12 disciples went on to pour themselves into many others, and they in turn raised up many sons and daughters. Jesus was one life, but He multiplied himself over and over again. We need to do that with those around us.

I remember years ago struggling with God, telling Him that I was only one person how could I ever make a difference? I think most people called into ministry probably have that conversation with God at one time or another. Suddenly, it was like God's words dropped on me like a heavy trench coat. I could hear myself say, "But God, I'm only one person."

One person does make a difference. Jesus was one person. He made a difference. Stop telling the Lord that the problem is too big. Stop looking at your problem. The more you look at the problem, the bigger it gets. God is bigger than that problem. Keep your eyes on God! Let God get bigger than your fears! You are one person, but you have the life of God on the inside of you. You can and will make a difference.

Chapter Twenty Two
The Anointed Eagles Vision

Vision released during a Waves of Revival Meeting in Belleville, IL.

Thank you Lord.

I had never seen this before but in the river that was in the midst of the vision this scripture was floating on top in letters. Exodus 19:4 says: And how I bear you on eagle's wings and brought you unto myself. And I'm telling you this is one of those profound details and it only happens when I'm in a trance- like state. In the vision I can see people around me. I can recognize what's going on. But I'm seeing a film that's going on while I'm looking. I could be looking at you and see in the spirit this thing unfolding and you're just kind of a vague picture that I can still see. And I'm telling you, it happens out of nowhere. It's not like I ask to get in. It's just like I start pressing into God and I got brought in, halleluiah. I was given this title and within a matter of moments I was taken into this trance-like state. We are moving into a season right now, going deep into the realm of the spirit and I'm talking about going deep into the realm of the spirit. My body was stationary but my spirit was moving. It was as though I was going from place to place with the Lord. I was on a journey toward something beautiful. The first thing I saw was a crystal clear river like Destin, Florida, where the ocean's so blue you can actually see the bottom of the ocean in most places. It's very beautiful, crystal clear, not blue, but clear and the water was very clear. It was flowing from a huge throne and the throne was so large that it appeared to have many levels. And I don't know what this means other than the throne that I believe was the throne of the Lord but at the same time it had many levels to it. It was much like a mountain, much like a progressive level of His throne. And it was as though we could climb it. But we couldn't and as I'm talking about it I can still see it. The river was very deep and it was flowing swiftly and I knew that somehow in these waters there was deliverance. There was freedom. And it's full of provision, in the river. And each level had to be fully finished. And we're going to be climbing later and it takes us to another level and another level and another level. We have to claim the provision from each level before we can go to the next level. There's a tangible anointing and glory released in the swirling of the water and I imagined by the Spirit as the water was swirling I was reminded in this trance that it was much like the pools of Bethesda being stirred by the angels. I saw an eagle flying. This eagle was pure white. A white eagle, in all aspects, from the head all the way even to the feet, everything was white. But it was an eagle. It was flying and I knew it was coming with a message. An eagle is like the prophet or the prophetic seeing anointing. Whenever God speaks to me He does it in this way. And God said this is the day that I'm going to release my message for my eagles. And I discern that the eagle was bringing a word of revelation for the Bride. And as I watched a white dove flying in over the churning waters join the eagle and the dove flew faster and faster following the eagle . Representation. The dove of course the Holy Spirit. The eagles are what God spoke in the soaking service. And it's just a minute piece of the puzzle that said we were going to rise up with wings of eagles. And all this time later God now is unfolding it because now we have crossed over into the next threshold. And a voice spoke and said: First comes the Prophet. And then the dove. I recognize this prophetic word because it had been spoken to me in prior visions. First comes the Prophet. Then comes the dove. The phrase prophet will help. You say, what does that mean? This was spoken to me when I had a vision many years ago, and William Branham, He's a minister that ministered and with evidence he had an angel that would stand beside him and that would speak words of knowledge into his ear and he would release those words of knowledge and people were healed by the masses. He was known as the prophet to our nation. If he said something all churches in our nation adjusted accordingly. And in the vision prior, this vision I'm talking about with William Branham. I had a vision and in the vision it was the picture where he's standing there and it looked like a halo but he said it was an angel standing beside him. And in that picture it's like he was frozen and he unfroze and he turned to me and he said Bill, I want people to take my mantel. I'm dead but my mantel's not. So I was reminded whenever it said here prophet with help. You see angels can speak to us. See, we only think we can see here, and understand, but understand it's not just hearing but also help and heavenly hosts to us as well. The voice continued to explain that the dove represented a true, genuine baptism of the Holy Spirit. How many know today we don't have a true Baptism of the Holy Spirit compared to what God really meant it to be. Now with the Holy Spirit means we should be walking in the miracles. So the next phase of this, I call it: the Bride wade out into the deeper revelation. We're the Bride by the way. I understood that the deep waters beckoning the Bride represented the profound revelations and mysteries, that the Bride of Christ has been called to walk in. God's word is being revealed, it is being revealed right now to her, in more intimate ways as the waters course over her. I was looking up again and I saw the eagle beginning to circle a large blue ball. I could see the shapes of the continents. I saw by the Spirit the continents all over the world. And I saw continents light up as the eagle was swarming around the world. As the eagle continued to circle the globe the white dove was following closely behind. Suddenly there appeared another bird, also in white color but it was a much larger bird. And then the dove. And it had the same body structure as an eagle, but his feathers were pure white, in another realm. I mean white that is white. The first eagle was white, but it was not white, white, white. It was like an off-white compared to the brightest white-white you could ever imagine. There was a glow about this eagle. It was like I said without saying: It's a white eagle!!!, another white eagle! An angel of the Lord appears. An angel stepped into the view dressed in white. I discerned that he was not an ordinary angel but he carried a high level of authority. I was sometimes able to communicate in the room with the angels without communicating. It's kind of a strange thing but sometimes I can do it. An angel asked me if I was familiar with his white eagle. The angel explained that it was more important for now that I just see him then to understand what he was there for. The angel then began to teach me about patience. I began to understand that God was dealing with me in like the simplicity of a small child, carefully repeating details as if I did not understand, when I understood. Carefully saying this is what this is for, this is what this is for, but He wasn't explaining the big eagle. If anything he was treating me like a little boy. They reminded me that the first eagle came leading the dove, a type of prophet leading the way, a true infilling of the Holy Spirit. Ephesians 1:13-14 In whom you also trusted after that which you heard the word of truth, the gospel of your salvation and who also after that you believed you were sealed with the Holy Spirit a promise which is the earnest of our inheritance until the redemption, the purchased possession unto the praise of His glory. As to the true infilling of the Holy Spirit but I believe the Lord was trying to describe in this vision. There's just another level of Pentecostal blessing and sensation that we haven't experienced yet. It's more than just fill. The baptism that's about to come upon us will not just produce another man made denomination or religious system but a genuine change in the life of a believer. Not added in this vision this time will be much different than any time in the world of the infilling of My Spirit. So in this time I was like so by this time I'm wading in the water and I said: I mean we're going to be filled with the Holy Spirit? He said right. And for the next weeks we're about to get filled, all over again. And it's going to be fresh and different. The disciples had already walked in miracles, already laid hands on people, seen miracles take place. And they asked that they might reach forth their hand to heal. They asked for boldness and they ended up getting filled again with the Holy Spirit. They were already filled. There's another level of filling. Remember the dove was following the eagle, the original eagle. Now the dove begins to lead the eagle. The angel of the Lord explained the true baptism of the Holy Spirit would prepare the way for the white eagle, the bright one that I never had the understanding of. And he said the white eagle represented a revelation of the fullness of Jesus Christ. Not just a greater knowledge of Him but an infilling, indwelling, of the very character and virtue of Jesus Christ. In other words, it was supposed to overtake the other eagle. So we were looking much like the white eagle but not quite like. They said He wants us to be one. We're going to make it. This revelation will produce a living word made flesh again. Not just one man Jesus Christ but many men and women of God rising up as anointed eagles. This message would act as a plumb line measuring device to gauge the uprightness of all the words given to the end time Bride of Jesus Christ. This is what we are being raised up to be, the end time Bride as eagles. I spoke out in those that I could see and I said the world has never seen what it will see in the Bride. And here's what God said: Fools will mock and reject it. Some religious leaders will scorn it, but His true Bride will receive it with gladness. The next thing, a new thing, (Isn't that what God's been speaking all this time?) God said it's time for the Bride's revival, the Bride's revival. I believe these words were referring to the Lord doing a new thing that will not follow historical revival patterns, but will have a distinct model and administration. It will be an expansion of the ministry model of Jesus Christ as seen in the gospels. It will be authority and power functioning and following in a corporate body of believers especially chosen for this purpose even before the foundation of the world. I then heard Him say something odd to me. Things are stuck on Mt. Zion. The Saints are stuck. They have climbed as far as they can and it seems they can't move any higher into the virtues and attitudes of Jesus. He added that I should not worry because it is not me to worry about them but just to worry about Him. Mt. Zion God said is on the back side of the throne. I said what does that mean and He says Mt. Zion is where everybody in the body of Christ has gone to get to. God says that's yesterday's glory. That's past tense. God says that's just the beginning of where I want to take My body. So it's behind the throne. What's before His throne is new levels that are above Mt. Zion. Suddenly before me what a beautiful pyramid shape and God said this is Mt. Zion. And I said, but God the last time I saw a pyramid in the Spirit it represented religion. God says yes. Mt. Zion has become a pyramid to the body of Christ. They can only climb so far and they are done. As I look closer I could see a mountain. Now the eagle is still moving around the blue ball of the continents and it's still got the Holy Spirit leading the eagle. And the other eagles are now becoming one and the throne that has many levels but then I look to the side. It's like you could climb the levels of the throne but God said that wasn't the way that we have to go. We have to climb the mountain. He said there's a mountain where it looked like you had to climb just little cliffs here and there and we had to climb. And I looked closer and I could see some saints. Some of you were in it. Scattered along the side of the mountain some had reached higher places than others but all were moving slowly toward the top. I was getting a closer look then I've ever had before and now I could see the roughness of the slopes and the rocky, jagged terrain. Small rocks would tumble off when people would grab them. In other words those rocks could cause you to fall. So every time, if you try to go too quickly you could fall. You had to make sure you were secure before you began to reach for a higher place. There's so many details. There are also large unstable boulders that would come from those that were above and those boulders would just roll over the top and you would have to hide yourself in the cleft of a rock.

Powerful. Otherwise you would be hit. Some climbers would be hit by these rocks, boulders and knocked to the bottom. Some would get back up and just start climbing again. Some had climbed to the place to where they were unable to navigate obstacles and some had to stop because there was no place to get a foothold any more or even dig in with their hands and pull themselves any higher. And I saw by the Spirit as I was seeing the difficulty that had begun to arise with many that were climbing this mountain. And more and more they were becoming stalled with no way around the hindrance it appeared, but most of them would be forced to retreat and re-navigate. The angel of the Lord startled my sadness for these people because he said don't worry. Remember just recently God told us in ministry: Don't wait for anyone. Just go. My whole life in ministry I have waited for every person to get it before we go to the next level and God said these last few months, He said don't wait anymore. Go. He said leave them. If they can't get to that next level just go. Let me worry about them. The dove releases new strength to climb. The most difficult climbing, they are going to be stranded for a long period of time. And with the right tools, it was as though on the mountain I could see tools appearing as the dove would swirl, to chisel out your next climbing spot. It took time to get out of your pit, your mess, your struggle, but if you use the tools you were able to dig yourself out. And if you did have to go down at all it was so that you could find another way out. Details. I saw a flash of movement overhead and it was the little white dove circling the top of the mountain. A fresh anointing began to shower down and I knew it was being released by the presence of the dove. Suddenly I saw a clear word that was imbedded in the stone of the face of the mountain and it said this: Eagle. It was as though somebody had carved in icicles the word Eagle. That's how I put it together "The Anointed Eagles." I heard the saints begin to shout and rejoice in the fresh anointing. Those that were defeated and down and could not move any more would begin to shout and say: We can do it now. Come on. We can do it. Come on. And I rejoiced with a fresh anointing and when it fell upon them like a blanket they started shouting to those below: We can make it. Keep on climbing. Someone replied. How do you know? Back up, as though they were trying to explain to them that worse was coming. Everyone could see the dove still circling the mountain. And in the distance someone else was approaching. As it drew closer someone shouted off the mountain. It's the white eagle, demonstrating the one eagle. And I was concerned about the saints standing at the bottom of the mountain and I felt that the lateness of the hour would make it impossible for them to make it to the top and I asked aloud: "How will they ever make it?" To those that did not give up. There were still bodies lying at the bottom who did give up. But to those who kept just saying, they may have been tired. They may have been weak. They may have been frustrated. But that eagle flew down and began to pick one by one up and take then to the next level. Jumping down the side of the mountain and near up to the top he drew in close nudging the saints, encouraging them to climb, and he would land them in another spot and kind of just hit them, like, come on. And God began to show me this eagle was no longer just the white, white eagle but this was the eagle that became one. I heard the eagle (I never heard an eagle talk but in this one the eagle got to talk.) When you have climbed as high as you can I will bear you on my wings to the top of Zion. And I asked the Lord. I said God you said Mt. Zion was just old stuff. He said Yes, this is a new Zion, a new place, a new level. The Bride will make it to the top. I will give her my virtues. I will carry her the rest of the way. Even as I bore Israel out of Egypt on my wings so I will carry you to the top of the mountain. I joined the other Saints in screaming: Eagle, just take us on your wings then. And I knew in my spirit that this would not constitute short cuts. The wings pick you up and take you over that lump but it doesn't take you all the way to the top. They might carry you to the top and show you what's up at the top but then He brings you back and puts you at the next level. You would not be able to by pass any of the lessons, preparations, and impartations. This bearing up would only happen in the hour when we could not climb any higher on our own. It would also have spoken of the end of all human striving to be qualified as over-comers. And a new place where we would finally emerge totally dependent on the Lord Jesus Christ. See the thing is this is not God given by-passes. And even carrying those who have given up. This is God who has nudged. He said don't worry. If they get left behind and they stay with Him in their heart, He's going to keep nudging them and pulling them a little higher. You say: Come on. You can do it. You can do it. I pray now that we're entering into a season of revelation that will lift us to the top of this new mountain top and cause us to be seated with our beloved Bridegroom in His throne. There's a new dimension He wants to take us. God says I want to anoint the eagles. We're the eagles. Thank you Lord! Halleluiah! All for the Glory of God!

Chapter Twenty Three
The Warrior Eagle Vision

I saw this Eagle that had a wing span beyond its normal wing span. The wing span seemed to go for miles from the left to the right. When the wings opened they seemed to go for miles. The Eagle's body was very strong and the head of the Eagle was a Dove's head. And on top of the Dove's head was a crown, a very beautiful crown was setting on the top of the Dove's head that is actually part of the Eagle. Within its mouth was a trumpet. And in the claw of the right hand of the Eagle was a gavel like a judge would use. And I saw this Eagle swarm down and go over a wheat field. And out of its wings flowed oil. Each piece and each part was very powerful but at the same time and then as I began to look in a little deeper it was like God would give me one piece and then I would see that for a while. And then he would add another piece to it and I saw the Eagle strapped to its body a giant sword. In the natural I began to think my goodness, this is just God showing Himself. But then I began to see that this Eagle was not flying alone. And all of a sudden I looked up and in a diamond shape just as the birds fly south for the winter there was a flock of these Eagles with the same crown, the same head, with the same gavels, and the same swords, and they produced hundreds if not thousands upon thousands, shaped as a diamond flying in the sky. And I heard the Lord say to me, that indeed I am raising up the Eagle warriors. They shall look like Me. They shall flow like Me. God said you are being advanced quickly. God says I want you to carry My crown. I want you to carry My supreme royalty. I want you to be led by My Spirit with the head always being in front. I want you to allow your mouth to blow the very trumpet, to sound alarms when needed. I want you to be able to spread your wings to release My anointing oil upon the harvest. I want you to be able to pull your sword at any given time, to sever the giants that are before the land. I want you to be releasing the very gavel of judgment upon the earth. That is where judgment needs to be made you're going to be My one to bring the hammer down, to say you have gone this far but you're not going any farther. The Lord says I'm raising up ones who will say YES! Don't think that this is a little thing. This is a very big thing of what God's speaking to, that we will walk in a level of authority and mantels beyond our supreme understanding. And I saw this Eagle flying over certain parts of the world. And the Eagles that were swarming together, they went in sync. The diamond shape of the Eagle's mass never separated. There was not one in disagreement if you see the birds flying south for the winter there seems like there's always a scatter somewhere or some birds eating French fries at a parking lot or something. You know they've stopped for this and they get out of sync. **But** in this picture it was in perfect sync and they were all in agreement together going the right direction because the head of the Holy Spirit was in front of every Eagle, being lead by the Spirit. So when they turned left they all turned left and when one stopped and hovered over a region- they all stopped and hovered over that region. Now the Lord spoke to my heart and He said I want you to consider this, when it says in My Word that **they** did signs and wonders. **They** flowed in miracles, signs, and wonders. The Lord says you shall be ones that even the very presence that I have in you shall be presence that hovers over and around My people. It was as though the people would gather together just waiting for the Eagles to take flight. People would gather together and wait for the Eagles to come over them, to fly over them. And I saw by the Spirit of God and the vision is even expanding as I'm telling it. Thank You Jesus. I saw out in the middle of the ocean much like the Air Force has landing ships that you can land out in the middle of the ocean. I saw Eagles coming down and landing on these ships and God says it's going to be considered chambers out in the waters. God says I'm going to do a movement out in the waters in the days ahead. Not on land. It will be out in the waters. It will be specifically for my people who are called by my name who are appointed for this hour. They will go there to get their sword sharpened. To get their spirits refreshed. To get the rest and the refreshing that is needed. And the Lord says these are going to be ones that will have revival on the water and then when they take flight again they'll come back stronger than they've ever been before, equipped more than they ever were before. And the Lord says this is not going to be one landing ship but many landing ships because it's going to have to be able to contain masses of these generals that God is raising up in this hour. The Lord says every Eagle will be as though Smith Wigglesworth, Kathryn Kuhlman, and all the great wonders of the world, are all combined in one because it's Jesus being reproduced of Himself. They are supposed to be flying high as Eagles. We're supposed to be able to walk in this kind of power and the Lord says you are receiving a greater anointing even now and I'm going to begin to plant my crowns upon thee. I'm going to begin to put the trumpets in your mouth to sound that alarm when needed. Halleluiah. And the Lord says I'm going to put the gavels in your hands and whenever somebody's being wrong by the way of the Spirit, you're going to put it down and say NO MORE and the Lord says this is going to be a strength that comes in numbers because the Lord says you're going to know who is just like you. You're going to be able to see it in the Spirit. For there will be many who will be just like you that you won't even know has been a part of it. They might have not been beside you, but they have in the Spirit says the Lord. Now all of a sudden I saw by the Spirit as these Eagles were flying - it's as though I saw one main Eagle that was flying in the midst of that and I know that represents Jesus Himself. But then all of a sudden it's like I saw shadows of Him spread out and it caused the masses of Eagles to be reproduced of Himself. Then I saw assignments being made upon Eagles and when they would take flight again they would go and I saw then they reproduced themselves. God says I don't want to just reproduce Myself, I want to reproduce yourself once you find yourself in Me says the Lord. When you're in Me and I am in you. And then I want you to be able to split off and the Lord says these are ones with the full mantels. These are ones with the full power. These are ones that can tap into My Spirit at any given moment and be able to do any wonder that is necessary for that time. And the Lord says it gets bigger and it gets bigger and it gets bigger. And there will come a day to where the Eagles shall gather. They shall gather in My name. They shall gather in places where I have not been before, because I'm going to cover the earth, is My promise, with My Glory. Don't think this is about titles. Don't think this is about position. This is about just being part of the whole mission that God has for us. **Sharpen! Sharpen** yourself in this hour. Sharpen your sword. Get ready for there's going to be a time that you are in flight for years at a time because you're going to go and go and go until I say it's time to land and get rest. For there are many Eagles says the Lord. My plan, says God, is to have one hundred thousand Eagles with this type of anointing with this type of power. They might not be all under the same type of denominational agreement. They might not be under the same type of ministry. They might not be under this title or that title. But they will be Eagles none the less because the Lord says I'm handpicking out of the remnant of people. The Lord says I will look down upon the body of Christ that may have a mass of hundreds and reach down and just pull one individual out of the whole mass who says yes. My children you have to understand that when you become this type of Eagle you can fall from a higher place. It's more vital than ever before that you, once you take flight you don't want to fall from that place, because it's from a higher place. God says someone can walk out the door and trip and fall and get their knee skinned. They can run off the top of the roof and break a leg. They can jump out of a certain plane and if they land just right they can just sever many bones in their body. But they can climb to the highest plain above the clouds in the unseen, that's a high place to where if you fall you die. You say Oh that's too much a burden to carry. I chose you. You did not choose Me. Many militant enlisted in the military with no desire to be a Green Beret but the Army chose them. Their desires were not to be that which they were chosen to be. They had special talent, a special ability, even a potential if you will that was seen within them to be chosen for this honor. God says I'm putting stripes on your shoulders, stripes of authority and position. This is why many of you have been rejected. You've been rejected by many; have been rejected by many moves, many advancements, many things. And the Lord says but I chose you specifically for this hour. And then I saw by the Spirit these Eagles were flying together. They were multi-colored, some, not one of them looked identical in color but they were identical in everything else. And God is saying by His Spirit, understand that you will have your own characteristics. Tap into this special anointing. There will be many different shades but they will all connect to the same and the Lord says. And some of you cry out "When does this begin?" NOW! "When does it start?" Right now. The Lord says you are only satisfied by fulfilling the high call that I have placed upon you. And there's no small thing of when I'm speaking of this. I have chosen you. You have been enlisted. Anything else would be a crime. Any other purpose in your life would be a crime. That would cause you to be court made Marshals by My Spirit. Can you handle it? Yes, I guarantee you can. Remember the head is the Dove. The Spirit shall guide you everywhere you go. When you start to lose heart the Spirit will lead you to the ship of rest, which is a natural thing, by the way. I'm not talking about that we will just enter into rest. God says there will actually be natural boats for rest, for restoration. Some of them will be as big as the Carnival Cruise lines specifically only for Eagles. God says just as many ships came as they discovered America. So shall many ships discover new heights in the realm of the Spirits. The Spirits, I said Spirits, the seven Spirits of God. The Lord says I'm going to begin to utilize you. And its going to seem like I've brutalized you. But the Lord says you're ready and you are well able. I did not choose the weak. I may have chosen the bashful. I may have chosen the shy. I may have chosen the nervous, racked with nervousness. I may have chosen the ones that say I will never do. But the Lord says NO means ON. And I shall shift you on this plan that I have. And whether you know it or not there's strength in this number. One day it may be 12 Eagles flying. And the next day it may be several 100. The next day it shall be several 1000. The shifting and changing that have taken place over the last years has been part of the promise being fulfilled. I, the Lord, knew Judas would fall when I chose him. So what's been done is what's in the past. I knew who would be ready today. I knew who I could use this way. I knew who would be ready to do all that I say. Do you see yourselves as kings? It is time for you to realize. Eagles, you shall see your reflections. Understand that when these Eagles are in flight there may be a leader. But there is the real leader: It's the Holy Spirit. So when you're in flight you're working as a well-oiled machine with all working parts, all movable parts. When one Eagle gets out of sync the whole plan gets messed up. And once these Eagles are in flight their lives aren't normal anymore. Green Berets have secret lives no one knows about. The FBI, CIA comes home and is not able to release one thing about what they have in the military, what they have in the Federal government. These Eagles shall have agreement in heaven where secrets will be revealed to them. And all of a sudden I just saw the Word of God written across the chest of Eagles. Some of you would say I don't really have the Word in me or I don't have the full Word upon me. The Lord says it's going to be branded upon you. You shall know things you should not know because the words are going to be branded on you like with a hot iron, a hot brand. I felt a little fear and trembling, a little worried, as I was releasing this in the room, because it's a high responsibility. I would not have chosen if I didn't think you were ready. Children are included in this. There are no small Eagles. There's no shape and size difference. There's no lesser brand. They don't make it a children's apple pie brand of the Word of God. It's the real Word of God seared upon their hearts. And the Lord says whether you know it or not I am making you ready. I am making you ready! Mighty warriors. I am making you ready. One of the last things that I need to really make sure that I get in here is that I saw the eyes of the Eagles in the Dove's head. They were flaming, literally moving fire. Somehow, some way I'm going to draw this picture. But the eyes were flaming, and as the eyes were flaming there was a flickering of flame in the eyes. They went back to their regular color. And I saw as Eagles would be flying over they would look down upon the earth in certain regions and all of a sudden their eyes would just like roll over into the flames of God. And God said it's the all-consuming fire. It's the fear of God. It's the authority within the eyes of the Lord. It's seeing with the piercing of dividing the soul and spirit. It's the supernatural convicting fire of God. It's that fire that's called the refiner's fire. It's that fire that releases fire. And the Lord says every Eagle shall have these eyes, eyes of fire, because this is what I need in this hour. For in the very end, says the Spirit of God, My word says that My eyes are going to be like fire. Just as My Eagles, My eyes are going to show through you, says the Spirit of God. I shall appear to many and I shall appear with healing in My wings. But if you are indeed supposed to be like Me and I the Lord am supposed to be like you, you in Me and I in you, shouldn't we have the same imagery. I'm making an army that shall look like Me. Some in this extreme, seem spooky and odd. Some have been considered the weird ones. Unless you fully embrace what I'm doing you haven't gotten odd yet. Ummm. Let's go another level. I saw by the Spirit as the Eagles would fly over certain regions, I saw dragons with fire coming out of their mouth. I saw beasts shooting at the Eagles. I saw serpents. I saw one that I would know was leviathan, python, all these spirits trying to attack and penetrate the very Eagles. And all of a sudden I saw as the Eagles were flying together and a lot of the enemy on the ground was trying to penetrate the very Eagles, trying to kill, trying to take them out. There were assignments against them to try to overtake them as they would come into certain regions. They more or less knew they were coming and they would try to penetrate. I saw the Eagles become transparent as they flew over. God says I'm causing stealth Eagles. And they shall fly and be able to be invisible when needed, not to be harmed. God says the full authority that I want to place upon these Eagles when they receive the fullness of this will be as though they are flowing in the strength and the power and the anointing much like Michael the Archangel. Warriors! And these are **humility** Eagles, because it's all about the One. The reason that the Dove stays at the head is because the Holy Spirit is always the guide, the head Eagle that's always God with healing in His wings. In other words they are more about Him than they are about themselves. The only thing of ourselves that shall be in the Eagle is the color. Everything else is about Him. Your own little piece of character, nature, and identity of who you are is the only part that's of that Eagle. Just as a Green Beret fighter, he is owned by the military. The military says I want you to go into the Middle East. I want you to capture so and so. They're ready! They don't second guess. They don't question it. They drop everything else and go. These warriors shall go when I say go. They shall take flight when I say take flight. They shall annihilate my enemy when seasons come to do so. Whether you know it or not these Eagles with the gavel, they understand that there will be, much like the slaying of the false prophets. Sounding the alarm will be as though they are slaying the enemy. The Lord says these Eagles will flow in an anointing beyond anointing and these will be flowing in the Spirit and power of Elijah and Moses. It's the supreme anointing of this last, last, last big bang of My authority and power. One day the Eagles by large number shall land around the White House here in the United States. And I see them raising their wings to cover the White House. And this is during the biggest shift of America giving up her full authority. The Eagles shall begin to protect what the White House stands for. I'm not talking about some president's home, some president's bowling alley, but God's saying for what this country represents the Eagles shall protect that. And even when governments begin to try to --- and I'm not talking about US governments, but other nations, governments try to overtake America's rights, the Eagles will continually protect the rights of America even when the government of the United States gives it up, for financial gain. It will look right. It will seem right. But it's part of the anti-Christ movement. And the Eagles shall be the last day prophets; a protection, an apostle, a protection of the very rights of America. And until the very last day before satan is sent to his pit, to be chained, never to be able to do anything again. My Eagles shall keep America believing red, white, and blue. It might just be a morsel of it. For the Lord says just as the measure of Israel, it has shrunk over the last 100 years piece by piece, chunk by chunk; the United States shall do the same, giving up this, giving up that. But the Lord says the very last, last, last thing that shall still result, that they will know that they know that they know that they are in the land of the free. I saw by the Spirit of God the Garden of Eden being restored at the very last in the Eagles. And it's as though it's in a dome of protection, in other words, the enemy cannot come in, sin is not allowed. It's only those who are friends of God that are allowed in this place' where the tree of life is, where the river of God is and God says this is going to be raised up and the last of the last. Because God says I'm restoring My Eden for My Eagles. We give You Praise. We give You Praise.

I want you to understand that when the Eagles spread their wings and go over the fields, the oil flows freely. There's no Eagle that will have less anointing than another. There might be a release differently but the oil will be plenty for all. These are Eagles of reproduction. These are Eagles of duplication. These are Eagles made in my real image. Are you ready for this? Some of you would say yes. And again I say are you ready for this? There will come a day just like some movie. You will be strapping on your boots; putting on your jacket; walking out the door; as though you were about to save the world. This is the type of warrior that I'm raising up in this hour. You will not need to fear death. You will not need to fear bullets, swords, or knives. Even bombing you will not have to fear. If you take hold the fullness of this I will be with you. And I will protect you. Do you receive this?

Some of you are probably caught a little off guard. I didn't know it was coming. God said: "Look," and I saw the Eagle. And it continued to unfold, even as I was releasing more unfolded, continuous vision. I could see you, but I could see the vision happening in front of you. It's like there's a transparency in the vision, where I could still see you there, continually flowing. And when God wants to show an image there's a reason why. There's really a reason. We need to understand. This is a critical hour, a very critical hour, because every Eagle had the trumpet. Every Eagle had the gavel. Every Eagle had the fire in their eyes. Every Eagle had the words upon its chest. Every Eagle had the anointing. Every Eagle had the wide span of wings that could cover for miles.

There's details in this some of you may have overlooked. Keep pressing into it so you can receive the whole picture. Some of you may want to write down each little thing and try to begin to expand the way God expanded on each little piece. And don't take this lightly. Some people are almost casual about this. Don't take it lightly, because this is the type of thing, that if you take it lightly you can fall. This is an assignment. You have been placed as special warriors. You have been placed to be mighty warriors. You didn't get picked because you were weak. You got picked because you have the potential to be great. This is not something you enlist. This is something you were enlisted. Embrace what God is saying. You have nothing to fear in this. Praise God, now and forever! All for Your Glory Lord!

About the Author

Bill Vincent is no stranger to understanding the power of God. Not only has he spent over twenty years as a Minister with a strong prophetic anointing, he is now also an Apostle and Author with Revival Waves of Glory Ministries in Litchfield, IL. Along with his wife, Tabitha, he, leads a team providing apostolic oversight in all aspects of ministry, including service, personal ministry and Godly character.

Bill offers a wide range of writings and teachings from deliverance, to experiencing presence of God and developing Apostolic cutting edge Church structure. Drawing on the power of the Holy Spirit through years of experience in Revival, Spiritual Sensitivity, and deliverance ministry, Bill now focuses mainly on pursuing the Presence of God and breaking the power of the devil off of people's lives.

His books 48 and counting has since helped many people to overcome the spirits and curses of Satan. For more information or to keep up with Bill's latest releases, please visit www.revivalwavesofgloryministries.com. To contact Bill, feel free to follow him on twitter @revivalwaves.

The Church is in a Season of Profound of Transition

Recommended Books

By Bill Vincent

Overcoming Obstacles

Glory: Pursuing God's Presence

Defeating the Demonic Realm

Increasing Your Prophetic Gift

Increase Your Anointing

Keys to Receiving Your Miracle

The Supernatural Realm

Waves of Revival

Increase of Revelation and Restoration

The Resurrection Power of God

Discerning Your Call of God

Apostolic Breakthrough

Glory: Increasing God's Presence

Love is Waiting – Don't Let Love Pass You By

The Healing Power of God

Glory: Expanding God's Presence

Transitioning to the Prototype Church

Receiving Personal Prophecy

Signs and Wonders

Signs and Wonders Revelations

Children Stories

The Rapture

The Secret Place of God's Power

Building a Prototype Church

Breakthrough of Spiritual Strongholds

Glory: Revival Presence of God

Overcoming the Power of Lust

Glory: Kingdom Presence of God

Transitioning to the Prototype Church

The Stronghold of Jezebel

Healing After Divorce

A Closer Relationship With God

Cover Up and Save Yourself

Desperate for God's Presence

The War for Spiritual Battles

Spiritual Leadership

The Church is in a Season of Profound of Transition

Global Warning

Millions of Churches

Destroying the Jezebel Spirit

Awakening of Miracles

Deception and Consequences Revealed

Are You a Follower of Christ

Don't Let the Enemy Steal from You!

A Godly Shaking

The Unsearchable Riches of Christ

Heaven's Court System

Satan's Open Doors

Armed for Battle

The Wrestler

Spiritual Warfare: Complete Collection

Growing In the Prophetic

Faith

The Angry Fighter's Story

Understanding Heaven's Court System

Web Site:

www.revivalwavesofgloryministries.com

The Church is in a Season of Profound of Transition

www.ingramcontent.com/pod-product-compliance
Lightning Source LLC
Chambersburg PA
CBHW052021070526
44584CB00016B/1844